Flannery O'Connor's Library:
Resources of Being

Flannery O'Connor's Library: Resources of Being

ARTHUR F. KINNEY

The University of Georgia Press   Athens

© 1985 by the University of Georgia Press
Athens, Georgia 30602
All rights reserved

Set in 10 on 13 Linotron 202 Palatino

Illustration of Flannery O'Connor
by Jack Coughlin

The paper in this book meets the guidelines for
permanence and durability of the Committee on
Production Guidelines for Book Longevity of the
Council on Library Resources.

Printed in the United States of America

88 87 86 85 84   5 4 3 2 1

Library of Congress Cataloging in Publication Data

Kinney, Arthur F., 1933–
    Flannery O'Connor's library.

    Includes bibliographical references and index.
    1. O'Connor, Flannery—Books and reading.
2. O'Connor, Flannery—Library—Catalogs.
I. O'Connor, Flannery.
II. Title.
PS3565.C57Z73 1985   813'.54   84-250
ISBN 0-8203-0726-2 (alk. paper)

We must remember that our state of contemplation must not be a state of inertia, but a state of preparation, a state in which we accumulate fervour, generosity, grace, so as to be ready and eager for any work to which the Lord may call us. We should be in our retirement like lions in their den; we should meditate in our house like taut bows, like wine in a bottle, like a force under pressure, so that in due time we may expand and burst forth.

Passage marked by Flannery O'Connor in her copy
of Claude Leetham, *Rosmini: Priest, Philosopher and Patriot*

Contents

Acknowledgments

I WOULD LIKE to extend once more my appreciation to the staff of the Ina Dillard Russell Library and the Flannery O'Connor Room at Georgia College, and especially to Gerald Becham, the curator at the time of my research, for their generous assistance through months of residence there, to the people of Milledgeville for their continuing hospitality, and to William Threadgill and Laynie Tzena Deutsch for their labor, counsel, and general acumen during every stage of research. T. S. J. G. Bögels assisted with the proofreading.

Introduction

OVER THE FLEETING YEARS of a brief life Flannery O'Connor assembled a rich and impressive collection of books on philosophy, theology, literature, and literary criticism at Andalusia, the family farmhouse just north of Milledgeville, Georgia. The signs of her frequent use of many of these books, her markings in them, and her references to them in a number of letters amply demonstrate their importance to her. Yet like everything else close to her—her mother, the farm, Catholicism, art—she could be desultory and derisive about her reading at the same time she was always, if indirectly, revealing. Concerning "the embarrassing subject of what I have not read and been influenced by," she wrote with gaiety to her close friend of later years, the anonymous "A.":

> I hope nobody ever asks me in public. If so I intend to look dark and mutter, "Henry James Henry James"—which will be the veriest lie, but no matter. I have not been influenced by the best . people. The only good things I read when I was a child were the Greek and Roman myths which I got out of a set of child's encyclopedia called *The Book of Knowledge*. The rest of what I read was Slop with a Capital S. The Slop period was followed by the Edgar Allan Poe period which lasted for years and consisted chiefly in a volume called *The Humerous Tales of E. A. Poe.* These were mighty humerous—one about a young man who was too vain to wear his glasses and consequently married his grandmother by accident; another about a fine figure of a man who in his room removed wooden arms, wooden legs, hair piece, artificial teeth, voice box, etc. etc.: another about the inmates of a lunatic asylum who take

over the establishment and run it to suit themselves. This is an influence I would rather not think about. I went to a progressive high school where one did not read if one did not wish to; I did not wish to (except the *Humerous Tales* etc.). In college I read works of social-science, so-called. The only thing that kept me from being a social-scientist was the grace of God and the fact that I couldn't remember the stuff but a few days after reading it.

I didn't really start to read until I went to Graduate School and then I began to read and write at the same time. When I went to Iowa I had never heard of Faulkner, Kafka, Joyce, much less read them. Then I began to read everything at once, so much so that I didn't have time I suppose to be influenced by any one writer. I read all the Catholic novelists, Mauriac, Bernanos, Bloy, Greene, Waugh; I read all the nuts like Djuna Barnes and Dorothy Richardson and Va. Woolf (unfair to the dear lady of course); I read the best Southern writers like Faulkner and the Tates, K. A. Porter, Eudora Welty and Peter Taylor; read the Russians, not Tolstoy so much but Dostoevsky, Turgenev, Chekhov and Gogol. I became a great admirer of Conrad and have read almost all his fiction. I have totally skipped such people as Dreiser, Anderson (except for a few stories) and Thomas Wolfe. I have learned something from Hawthorne, Flaubert, Balzac and something from Kafka, though I have never been able to finish one of his novels. I've read almost all of Henry James—from a sense of High Duty and because when I read James I feel something is happening to me, in slow motion but happening nevertheless. I admire Dr. Johnson's *Lives of the Poets*. But always the largest thing that looms up is *The Humerous Tales of Edgar Allan Poe*. I am sure he wrote them all while drunk too.[1]

Flannery kept the books she prized behind the glass doors of two large, handsome Victorian bookcases made of Georgia walnut in or near Savannah, which she had known first in the home of Mrs. Raphael Semmes, "Cousin Katie," whose house and garden adjoined her childhood home at 207 East Charlton Street in Savannah, just across the square from and under the appropriate shadow of the Cathedral of John the Baptist. She bought these bookcases at a family sale and had them shipped, at considerable expense, to Milledgeville. She was overjoyed with the purchase. "You must come again soon and see these bookcases. They are so big that they have drained most of what is in my room and those now stand ready to be refilled," she told "A." in June 1962.[2] They had a pronounced effect; a year later, writing Janet McKane, she alluded almost casually to "the library I'm building up. When I die I'm going to leave this to the city library, a good Catholic collection for this good Protestant town."[3] By then she was in the habit of ordering books from Modern Library—good value for money; and she ticked off in some of her volumes other titles she wished to buy as well as recording those she already owned. This process replaced the earlier practice of ordering from the Cross Currents Bookstore where, she reported to "A.": "I buy books . . . because they give me a 20% discount, which is quite a lot, and you don't have to pay the tax. What I should have done is to have ordered the books from England. English books are much cheaper even with the postage. I get lists from Peter Russell, an English 2nd hand place and I will pass them on to you if you would be interested. I am like the little boy who just liked to *feel* candy; I like to read booklists."[4]

She also liked to read the books themselves. At first, dates of acquisition tell us, she read for thesis and technique; her markings in her books are frequent and often directly related to her own work already underway. Later, she continued her heavy load of reading in order to compose book reviews; she wrote for her diocesan paper and thought of it as her special gift of charity. Many of these books she loaned or gave to friends; but many, too, she preserved in her own "good Catholic collection."

Yet this collection can also seem an accumulated jumble. When we come to examine at close range the library Flannery O'Connor left, given by her mother to the Ina Dillard Russell Library of Georgia College when the Mary Vinson Library of Milledgeville turned out to be too small and crowded to house it, we find the results somewhat mixed. She kept as treasures from her earliest years, for instance, certain textbooks—a later edition of *Understanding Fiction*, but original copies of *The Story Survey, The Divine Comedy, Political and Social Growth of the American People*—and while their markings often convey schoolroom assignments they also tell us how she approached them and how others instructed her in them. Other books are gifts of friends, admirers, or publishers; some with pages still uncut, some nearly new and apparently unused. Still others are the books she ordered, books she studied—like the letters and notebooks of Henry James, Percy Lubbock's *The Craft of Fiction*, and novels she ordered from Modern Library. As she commented in her letters, there seemed to be "God's plenty of Conrad, of Hawthorne (and on him), and of Mauriac."

What is problematic are those books *not* in the collection. Only 90 of the 130 books she reviewed are accounted for; missing are such various works as Stephen Vincent Benét's *Selected Letters*, William Clancy's *Religion and the Free Society*, Sister Emily Daly's *Joseph, Son of David*, V. M. Woodgate's *Saint Vincent de Paul*, Paul Horgan's *Give Me Possession* and *Humble Powers*, Evelyn Waugh's *The Ordeal of Gilbert Pinfold*, and J. F. Powers's *The Presence of Grace*.[5] We do not know how extensively she marked them—or whether they were finally of little importance and discarded (or of much importance and shared with friends). Collections of *The Critic, Cross Currents, The Georgia Review*, and *Jubilee*, which she reviewed, are missing for the most part. Books for which she wrote commentaries to be used on dust jackets—Robie Macauley's *The End of Pity and Other Stories* (1957), John Hawkes's *The Lime Twig* (1961), Françoise Mallet-Joris's *The Favourite—A Novel of the Court of Louis XIII* (1962), Cecil Dawkins's *The Quiet Enemy* (1963), and Richard Stern's *Teeth, Dying and Other Matters* (1964)— are not to be found in the collection.

Nor are various titles there which she mentions as of some interest in her letters, such as *The Idiot, Ship of Fools, The Hamlet, Journey to the End of Night, The Spoils of Poynton, The Deer Park, Magister Ludi, Idiots First*, three novels of Joyce Cary, and, among works of nonfiction, Frank O'Connor's *The Mirror in the Roadway*, Allen Tate's *The Man of Letters in the Modern World*, Mario Praz's *The Romantic Agony*, and Samuel Beckett's *Proust*. Sally Fitzgerald remembers a lost but annotated copy of Jacques Maritain's *Art and Scholasticism* which she replaced,[6] while Robert Giroux recalls an autographed copy of Thomas Merton's *Prometheus: A Meditation* that is now wanting.[7] In a visit to Andalusia shortly after O'Connor's death, Sister Kathleen Feeley examined not only William F. Lynch's *Christ and Apollo* but George Burchett's *Memoir of a Tattooist*, edited by Peter Leighton, which doubtless played a part in the composition of "Parker's Back," but neither is in the O'Connor Room collection. Besides the known books unaccounted for, there are the unknown ones; she alluded in her letters to the fact that "A." frequently sent her books on loan from a library in Atlanta,[8] and she borrowed a great many as well from the library of her alma mater through the auspices of Elizabeth Ferguson, a good friend who was the college reference librarian at the time and who kindly obtained any book O'Connor needed or wanted to read. Still she may have loaned other books that have never been returned. What is most startling of all are the fundamental omissions. We find in the library now housed at Georgia College no Chaucer, Shakespeare, or Milton; no Austen, Brontë, Flaubert, or Hardy, and precious little Dickens; no Southern fiction by Glasgow, Percy, Styron, or Warren, although Sally Fitzgerald reports that such books are still privately held at Andalusia.

Still, even to acknowledge such lacunae does not begin to tarnish the richness of what we still have. By our standards, she owned many books and kept them unusually well, with dust jackets intact even with heavy usage, and she talked to them, drawing lines in the margins, underlining, starring passages, checking (and even numbering) points seriatim, and writing marginalia of agreement, joy, bafflement, irritation, scorn, or mockery. Together they illuminate the shape of her mind and some essential components of her reading interests. Singly, they lead us to ideas, images, and fine points of aesthetics that were already evident in her work for those who were aware of them. In providing a context for her fiction they are priceless, for they point out where she found confirmation, enlargement, or definition of what she had previously observed and imagined in concrete human experience.

As for the contents of the present collection, it is perhaps the reflection of her staunch Catholicism that is most impressive. "She was a keen amateur theologian," Sister Kathleen Feeley concluded, "and owned one of the finest private theological libraries in this country."[9] Her concentration was in the major French and German theologians of the Roman Church—in Maritain, Gilson, Bloy, Peguy, Marcel, and Weigel—as well as in the American Lynch and the non-Catholics Barth and Buber. She enjoyed a special emphasis in studies of the Bible, both learned and lay,[10] saints' lives and commentaries, and the work of Teilhard de Chardin; she followed mysticism into the psychology of religion (with Emmanuel Mounier, Victor White, and William James) and even into Zen Buddhism. Her gathering of studies in Church history incorporated work on the Protestant Reformation and on Hebrew thought and Greek philosophy.[11] The collection also contains works by popular Catholic scholar and exegete Ronald Knox, although she never marked his books the way she underscored other books she owned. Her interest in Catholic writings extended to the novelists also—to Bernanos here, and to Gordon, Mauriac, Powers, and Waugh.

Of even more pointed interest are the marginalia which are direct signposts. Reading Mounier's *Personalism* after writing her second novel with its title drawn from the New Testament, she wrote that title, "the violent bear it away," in the margin alongside this passage:

> Love is a struggle: life is a struggle against death; spiritual life is a struggle against the inertia of matter and the sloth of the body. The person attains self-consciousness, not through some ecstasy, but

by force of mortal combat; and force is one of its principal attributes. Not the brute force of mere power and aggression, in which
man forsakes his own action and imitates the behaviour of matter;
but human force, which is at once internal and efficacious, spiritual and manifest. Christian moralists used to give this dimension
to their conception of fortitude, and the great aim of this fortitude
was to overcome the fear of bodily evil—and beyond that, of
death, the supreme physical disaster. For the lack of moral courage is often, quite stupidly, a fear of being hit. Moreover, they
related fortitude to liberality and magnanimity; i.e., to generosity
of nature: many are made cowardly to avarice and by lack of
imagination. It is always an internal victory over death that re-
unites these two fields of energy: a person only comes to full
maturity at the moment when he is seized of loyalties he values
more than life itself. But in modern conditions of comfort and of
indulgent care for the feelings, we have long cultivated, under the
cover of philosophies of love and of peace, the most monstrous
misunderstandings of these elementary truths.

O'Connor's frequent use of sun imagery has called forth much
critical commentary on the sun as God or the eye of God, but we
get a further extension of meaning from a passage she marked in
a study on St. Bonaventure that reads, "From the theological
tradition St. Bonaventure received the Augustinian principle
that the Word is the Sun of the mind, the light thanks to which
created spirits are able to see intellectually."

From other passages that she thought worth marking, as if
for emphasis and for later reference, we can piece together parts
of her aesthetic theory; see, for example, the annotations to
Edmund Fuller, Lord David Cecil, Emmanuel Mounier, Jacques
Maritain, St. Thomas Aquinas, and Alexis de Tocqueville, and,
more predictably, to Carl Jung, Percy Lubbock, Henry James,
Richard Chase, and Nathaniel Hawthorne. Together they lead
to what William Lynch perceptively calls "a theology of creativity."[12] She found other support in passages in Barth, Rabut,
Newman, Leetham, Guardini, and Eliade, while her under-

standing of the prophet owes something to her bracketed passage in Voegelin's *World of the Polis:* "The leap in being entails the obligations to communicate and to listen. Revelation and response are not a man's private affair; for the revelation comes to one man for all men, and in his response he is the representative of mankind. And since the response is representative it endows the recipient of revelation, in relation to his fellow men, with the authority of the prophet."

Other possible connections are even more particular, such as those penciled portions that relate to *Wise Blood* (catalog entries 46, 51, 71, 241, 385), to *The Violent Bear It Away* (51, 61, 98, 100, 242), and to her stories—to "Greenleaf" (57), to "The Lame Shall Enter First" (57, 332), to "The Enduring Chill" (59, 150), to "Revelation" (60), to "A Temple of the Holy Ghost" (61, 103), to "The River" (75, 196, 268), to "Everything That Rises Must Converge" (96), to "The Displaced Person" (117, 454), to "A Good Man Is Hard to Find" (132, 252), to "Good Country People" (137), to "The Turkey" (149), to "The Comforts of Home" (242), to "The Artificial Nigger" (267), to "The Life You Save May Be Your Own" (152), and to "Judgment Day" (388). Such a list is suggestive, not exhaustive; surely the joy of leafing through this catalog, and her books, is encountering (with shocks of recognition) passages that call up resonances from O'Connor's memorable fiction. What is illuminated here for the discerning reader are the fundamental dimensions of O'Connor's thought and art: this listing of her personal books demonstrates conclusively the seriousness of her writing, the logic of her thinking, and the fineness of her sensibility. Here too, among her books, Flannery O'Connor stands before us.

Notes

1 Sally Fitzgerald, ed., *The Habit of Being: The Letters of Flannery O'Connor* (New York: Farrar, Straus and Giroux, 1979), pp. 98–99.
2 Ibid., p. 478.

3   Ibid., p. 527.
4   Ibid., p. 109.
5   Lorine M. Getz, *Flannery O'Connor: Her Life, Library and Book Reviews*, vol. 5 of *Studies in Women and Religion* (New York: Edwin Mellen Press, 1980), gives a full listing.
6   Fitzgerald, *Letters*, p. xvii.
7   Robert Giroux, Introduction to *Flannery O'Connor: The Complete Stories* (New York: Farrar, Straus and Giroux, 1971), p. xiv.
8   Fitzgerald, *Letters*, p. 107.
9   Sister Kathleen Feeley, *Flannery O'Connor: Voice of the Peacock* (New Brunswick, N.J.: Rutgers University Press, 1972), p. xii.
10 See Getz, *Flannery O'Connor: Her Life, Library and Book Reviews*, pp. 72–73.
11 Fitzgerald, *Letters*, p. 306.
12 In addition to these annotations, see entries 271, 272, 275, 387, and others.

Notes on the Catalog

THE FOLLOWING LIST of Flannery O'Connor's books includes the entire holdings of her library now housed in the O'Connor Memorial Room (opened in 1974) at the Ina Dillard Russell Library of Georgia College in Milledgeville. The ordering follows that of the collection as it is presently shelved by the Dewey Decimal System, which shows at once the concentrations of her holdings (theology, fiction) and which brings together related books (Biblical studies, saints' lives), although following Dewey entries can sometimes result in peculiar double listings (see, for example, entries 148 and 149). This ordering does not reflect O'Connor's specific arrangement of books, since several family members rearranged some of the books between the time of her death and their accession to the Russell Library, but the rough general divisions of philosophy, theology, history, literature, and literary criticism are hers. Journals and magazines, which are stored separately in the O'Connor Room, are listed as a separate division. One of O'Connor's friends sent her a number of magazines in the last years of her life, and she might have retained copies that, in better health and at another time, she would have discarded. A subsequent register of names in the Index effectually offers a different catalog by name of author and points out those writers who form the core of her collection, bringing together variant listings of a single author (such as Bouyer) whose names vary in the catalog following the title pages of the works listed.

All the books are hardback (unless designated "Pap.," paperback) with dust jackets (unless indicated as having a plasticine wrap or being "W/o dj," without dust jacket). The name of the publisher and the place and date of publication of O'Connor's copy are given, along with a listing of any series designation, any editorial matter, and—if the original place of publication was different or the date of publication more than two years previous at the same place—these are supplied in parentheses. Conjectural material (such as a publication date conjectured from the copyright date) is given in brackets. The fullness of the information is meant to allow readers to consult copies close to home and know that they are (or are not) examining copies identical to those on which pagination for marginalia is given. Editorial information is presented, since O'Connor may well have studied editorial comments, as we know she read the prefaces by Warren (in entries 302, 330, 508, and 600). "N.p." indicates that no publisher's name is given (or no place of publication); "n.d." indicates that no date of publication is supplied.

Following such matters of bibliography, acknowledgment is made of her markings. Unless noted, "signed" means O'Connor wrote her name as "F. O'Connor," with or without a date as indicated, but except for the variant "Mary Flannery O'Connor" or "M. F. O'Connor," which denote early ownership, no special meaning can be attached to her signature except, of course, her intention to keep the book as a permanent part of her library. "Marginal lining" indicates a vertical line in the outside margin of a page; in making these, O'Connor was always careful to begin the line at the start of a sentence or phrase and to end it at the conclusion of the idea she meant to record. Underlining, check marks (usually in the margin), and asterisks are likewise listed, while marginalia—of whatever sort that met her eye each time she opened the book—are next. In recording such markings, a hyphenated reference (as in "pp. 278–79") notes that the marking is of one continuous passage; separate passages are separately listed (for example, "pp. 278, 279"). The more important passages—slightly more than half—have been transcribed in full, if there is a clear relationship between that material and her thought or writings. In all citations by O'Connor, the original form and spelling have been preserved. On rare occasions, O'Connor's markings stopped in midsentence; in those instances, I have completed the sentence in the extracts reprinted here.

Finally, published reviews of a given title are noted by an abbreviation of the name of the publication and its date, and reviews which we know she wrote but did not publish in her lifetime are designated "review unpublished." Her reviews appeared in *The Bulletin* and *The Southern Cross*, published successively by the diocese of Savannah; *Catholic Week;* and *American Scholar*. Page references for *Reviews* are to *The Presence of Grace and Other Book Reviews by Flannery O'Connor*, compiled by Leo J. Zuber and edited by Carter W. Martin (Athens: University of Georgia Press, 1983). Early references to some of these reviews, as well as references to parts of O'Connor's library, may be found in Sister Kathleen Feeley, *Flannery O'Connor: Voice of the Peacock* (New Brunswick, N.J.: Rutgers University Press, 1972), although they are, on occasion, inaccurate. References to O'Connor's *Letters*, which include any mention of a particular book, its preparation, publication, reception, or the ideas in it and O'Connor's evaluation of it, are to *The Habit of Being: The Letters of Flannery O'Connor*, edited by Sally Fitzgerald (New York: Farrar, Straus and Giroux, 1979).

Flannery O'Connor's Library

General

1 WOOLF, VIRGINIA. *Hours in a Library.* Prefatory note by Leonard Woolf. New York: Harcourt, Brace, [1957]. 24 pp. Plasticine wrap.

   Frontispiece is from a photograph of Virginia Woolf at age twenty. "This essay, one of a new group of essays by Virginia Woolf, has been privately printed for the friends of the publishers as a New Year's greeting."

Philosophy

2 D'ARCY, MARTIN C., S.J. *The Meeting of Love and Knowledge: Perennial Wisdom.* World Perspectives Series, preface by Ruth Nanda Anshen, vol. 15. New York: Harper and Brothers, [1957]. 167 + xix pp.

   Bulletin, 4.5.58; *Reviews,* pp. 54–55.

3 MARITAIN, JACQUES. *The Range of Reason.* Scribner Library SL 47. New York: Charles Scribner's Sons, 1952. 227 + xii pp. Pap.

   Bulletin, 11.25.61; *Reviews,* pp. 124–25.

4 GILSON, ETIENNE. *The Unity of Philosophical Experience.* Foreword by Gilson. New York: Charles Scribner's Sons, 1952 [New York, 1937]. 331 + vii pp.

   Marginal lining, p. 37.

   Letters, pp. 107, 477.

5 MARCEL, GABRIEL. *Metaphysical Journal.* Trans. Bernard

Wall. Chicago: Henry Regnery, 1952 (Paris, 1927). 344 + xiii pp.

    Signed, dated 1955.

    Letters, pp. 59, 463.

6 ———. *The Mystery of Being*. Vol. 1, *Reflection and Mystery*, trans. G. S. Fraser. Chicago: Henry Regnery, n.d. (London, 1950). 219 + xiv pp.

    The first of two series of Gifford Lectures given by Marcel in 1949 and 1950 at the University of Aberdeen.

    Signed, dated 1953. Marginal marking, top p. 34.

    Letters, pp. 94, 296–97, 299, 463.

7 ———. *The Mystery of Being*. Vol. 2, *Faith and Reality*, trans. René Hague. Chicago: Henry Regnery, n.d. (London, 1951). 188 + viii pp.

    The second of two series of Gifford Lectures given by Marcel in 1949 and 1950 at the University of Aberdeen.

    Signed, dated June 1953.

8 MARITAIN, JACQUES. *A Preface to Metaphysics: Seven Lectures on Being*. New York: New American Library, Mentor Omega MP 403, 1962. 142 pp. Pap.

9 BERGSON, HENRI. *The Creative Mind: An Introduction to Metaphysics*. Trans. Mabelle L. Andison. Wisdom Library. New York: Philosophical Library, 1946. 252 pp. Pap.

    Two new lectures and previously published material.

10 BOAS, GEORGE. *The Limits of Reason*. Religious Perspectives, ed. Ruth Nanda Anshen, vol. 3. New York: Harper and Brothers, 1961. 162 pp.

11 COLLINS, JAMES. *The Existentialists: A Critical Study*. Chicago: Henry Regnery, 1952. 268 pp.

    Signed, dated 1954.

12 LEWIS, C. S. *The Problem of Pain*. New York: Macmillan MP 120, 1962 (1940). 160 pp. Pap.

13 MUMFORD, LEWIS. *Man as Interpreter*. New York: Harcourt, Brace, 1950. 17 pp. Plasticine wrap.

    Portion of *The Conduct of Life*. "This first edition of *Man as*

Interpreter is privately printed for the friends of the author and his publishers as a New Year's greeting."

14 TEILHARD DE CHARDIN, PIERRE. *The Phenomenon of Man.* Trans. Bernard Wall. Introduction by Sir Julian Huxley. New York: Harper and Brothers, 1959; *Le Phénomène Humain* (Paris, 1955). 318 pp.

Signed, dated 1959. Marginal linings, pp. 19, 180, 218–19. Marginalia: "*inexperiential **praetor-experiential," p. 99. "A developed human being, as he rightly pointed out, is not merely a more highly individualized individual. He has crossed the threshold of self-consciousness to a new mode of thought, and as a result has achieved some degree of conscious integration—integration of the self with the outer world of men and nature, integration of the separate elements of the self with each other" (marginal lining, p. 19).

Bulletin, 2.20.60; *American Scholar* 30 (Fall 1961): 618; *Reviews*, pp. 129–30; *Letters*, pp. 361, 368, 383, 387–88, 438, 449, 477.

15 LYNCH, WILLIAM F., S.J. *The Integrating Mind: An Exploration into Western Thought.* New York: Sheed and Ward, 1962. 181 pp. W/o dj.

Marginal linings: pp. 24, 26, 32, 37, 45, 55, 99.
Bulletin, 8.4.62; *Reviews*, pp. 146–47.

16 D'ARCY, M. C., S.J. *The Nature of Belief.* New introduction by D'Arcy. St. Louis: B. Herder, 1958 (Dublin, 1931). 236 pp.

Marginal lining, p. 102.
Bulletin, 1.24.59; *Reviews*, p. 67.

17 JUNG, C. G. *The Undiscovered Self.* Trans. R. F. C. Hull. New York: New American Library, Mentor MD 259, 1959. 125 pp. Pap.

Marginal linings: pp. 69, 72, 107. Marginalia: "Teilhard?" pp. 92, 103; "Teilhard," p. 123.
Letters, pp. 362–63, 394.

18 MOUNIER, EMMANUEL. *The Character of Man.* Trans. Cynthia

Rowland. Abridged text. New York: Harper and Brothers, 1956. 341 pp.

Signed, dated 1957. Marginal linings on pp. 4, 5, 6, 12, 13, 14, 15, 17, 18, 24, 35, 36, 70, 73, 79, 80, 84, 98, 119, 122, 177, 179, 213, 219, 221, 247, 252, 253, 281, 304. Underlining: pp. 246, 273. Marginalia: "simultaneous attraction–repulsion," p. 19; "nemo," p. 118; "vs Hopkins inscape?" p. 224; "Hopkins inscape," p. 224; "D. H. Lawrence?" p. 256; "Mauriac *Destinies*," p. 272; "Destins," p. 274.

"No character has been restored to its metapsychological background, it transfers the stress from the given to the willed, or more exactly, from determination, to a personally directed choice. My character is not what I am in the sense of a snapshot registering all past determinations, all the features already formed. It is the form of a greater movement directed towards the future, and concerned with greater fullness of being. It is what I can be rather than what I am, my availability rather than my possessions, the hope that is still open rather than the achievements I have left behind. 'What is truest of an individual, and the most himself, is his possibility, that is only shown indistinctly in his history' " (marginal lining, p. 15).

"Character is not a fact, but an act" (marginal arrow and underlined, p. 17).

"When we say that thought is dialogue, we mean this quite strictly. We never think alone. The unspoken thought is a dialogue with someone who questions, contradicts, or spurs one on. This inner debate, however complicated and prolonged—it may last a lifetime—is quite different from rumination, which is a wandering around the same spot. Even if immobilized by crises from time to time, the inner dialogue moves towards an aim. It is, in spite of its interiorization, realistic thought. Its coherence is made of social encounters and solid experience. It has the same pattern as the elementary behaviour

of thought, which is both *conversation* and *meditation*"
(marginal lining, p. 252).

> *Bulletin*, 10.16.57; *Reviews*, pp. 44–45.

19 PICARD, MAX. *The World of Silence* (*Die Welt des Schweigens*).
Trans. Stanley Godman. Preface by Gabriel Marcel. Humanist Library. Chicago: Henry Regnery, 1952. 231 pp.

> Signed, dated 1952. Marginal linings, pp. 13, 33, 41.

20 WIESINGER, ALOIS, O.C.S.O. *Occult Phenomena in the Light of
Theology*. Trans. Brian Battershaw. Westminster, Md.: Newman Press, 1957. 294 + xvi pp.

> Signed, dated March 1957. Marginal linings on pp. 141,
> 195.
>
> *Bulletin*, 6.8.57; *Reviews*, pp. 38–39.

21 MESEGUER, PEDRO, S.J. *The Secret of Dreams* (*El Secreto de los
Sueños*). Trans. Paul Burns. Westminster, Md.: Newman Press, 1960. 232 pp.

> Signed, dated 1960. Marginal lining on p. 37.
>
> *Letters*, p. 412.

22 BERGSON, HENRI. *The World of Dreams*. Trans. Wade Baskin.
New York: Philosophical Library, 1958. 58 pp.

23 MOUNIER, EMMANUEL. *Personalism*. Trans. Philip Mairet.
New York: Grove Press, 1952; *Le Personnalisme* (Paris, 1950).
132 + xx pp. Plasticine wrap.

> Marginal linings on pp. 49, 80, 81. Marginalia: "the violent
> bear it away," p. 49, with marginal marking of this passage:
> "Love is a struggle: life is a struggle against death; spiritual
> life is a struggle against the inertia of matter and the sloth of
> the body. The person attains self-consciousness, not
> through some ecstasy, but by force of mortal combat; and
> force is one of its principal attributes. Not the brute force of
> mere power and aggression, in which man forsakes his own
> action and imitates the behaviour of matter; but human
> force, which is at once internal and efficacious, spiritual and
> manifest. Christian moralists used to give this dimension to
> their conception of fortitude, and the great aim of this forti-

tude was to overcome the fear of bodily evil—and beyond that, of death, the supreme physical disaster. For the lack of moral courage is often, quite stupidly, a fear of being hit. Moreover, they related fortitude to liberality and magnanimity; i.e., to generosity of nature: many are made cowardly by avarice and by lack of imagination. It is always an internal victory over death that re-unites these two fields of energy: a person only comes to full maturity at the moment when he is seized of loyalties he values more than life itself. But in modern conditions of comfort and of indulgent care for the feelings, we have long cultivated, under the cover of philosophies of love and of peace, the most monstrous misunderstandings of these elementary truths."

24 HEIDEGGER, MARTIN. *Existence and Being*. Foreword by Stefan Schimanski. Introduction by Werner Brock. Chicago: Henry Regnery, 1949. 399 pp.

  Signed, dated August 1954. Marginal lining on p. 359.

  Letters, pp. 243, 251.

25 PIEPER, JOSEF. *Leisure: The Basis of Culture* (*Musse und Kult* and *Was Heisst Philosophieren?*). Trans. Alexander Dru. Introduction by T. S. Eliot. New York: Pantheon, 1954 (New York, 1952). [169] pp.

26 SHRADY, M. L., ED. *Come, South Wind: A Collection of Contemplatives*. Introduction by Martin C. D'Arcy, S.J. New York: Pantheon, 1957. 158 pp.

  Bulletin, 2.28.58; *Reviews*, pp. 53–54.

27 MARITAIN, JACQUES. *Creative Intuition in Art and Poetry*. New York: Meridian M8, 1955 (1953). 334 pp. Pap.

  "This is the first volume of the A. W. Mellon Lectures in the Fine Arts, which are delivered annually at the National Gallery of Art, Washington."

  Marginal linings on pp. 123, 148. Underlining: pp. 126, 146, 151, 162, 164–65.

  "We may observe at this point that art endeavors to imitate in its own way the conditions peculiar to the pure spirits: it draws beauty from ugly things and monsters, it tries to overcome the division between beautiful and ugly by absorbing ugliness in a superior species of beauty, and by transferring us *beyond* the (aesthetic) beautiful and ugly" (underlined, p. 126).

"St. Thomas insisted that art imitates nature *in her operation*—not in respect to natural appearances, but in respect to the ways in which nature herself operates" (underlined, pp. 164–65).

28 NEUMANN, ERICH. *The Origins and History of Consciousness*. Bollingen Series, trans. R. F. C. Hull, vol. 42. Foreword by C. G. Jung. New York: Pantheon, 1954; *Ursprungsgeschichte des Bewusstseins* (Zurich, 1949). 493 + xxiv pp. Illus.

Signed, dated June 1955.

Letters, p. 103.

29 RIESMAN, DAVID, NATHAN GLAZER, AND REUEL DENNEY. *The Lonely Crowd: A Study of the Changing American Character*. Abridged text. New York: Doubleday, Anchor A16, 1953 (New Haven, Conn., 1950). 359 pp. Pap.

30 LUBAC, HENRI DE, S.J. *Further Paradoxes* (*Nouveaux Paradoxes*). Trans. Ernest Beaumont. Westminster, Md.: Newman Press, 1958. 128 + x pp.

Marginal linings on pp. 5, 9, 13.

"As the life of the spirit develops, it inevitably comes up against new data, giving rise to new problems. New thresholds appear, which must be crossed, without our knowing into what new domains we shall be forced to enter. Drawing back or stopping even is impossible. That would not be showing humility, but giving up; not firmness, but bewilderment; not security, but suicide. So all spiritual life, that of the intelligence like that of the soul, calls for a share of adventure. All tradition requires the finding of new things. For the intelligence as well as for the soul, fidelity is of necessity creative" (marginal lining, p. 13).

Bulletin, 10.4.58; *Reviews*, pp. 58–59.

31 TRESMONTANT, CLAUDE. *Pierre Teilhard de Chardin: His Thought (Introduction à la pensée de Pierre Teilhard de Chardin).* Trans. Salvator Attansio. Preface by Gustave Weigel, S.J. Baltimore: Helicon Press, 1959. 128 + viii pp.
Signed, dated 1960. Marginal notations on pp. 36, 42, 43, 44, 48, 49, 67, 70, 78, 80, 81, 82, 84–85, 86, 87, 88, 94. Review unpublished; *Letters,* pp. 334, 388.

32 ———. *A Study of Hebrew Thought (Essai sur la Pensée Hébraïque).* Trans. Michael Francis Gibson. Foreword by John M. Oesterreicher. New York: Desclee, 1960. 178 + xx pp.
Signed, dated 1960. Marginal notations on pp. xii, 11, 46, 58, 97, 98, 99, 100, 101, 108, 109. Marginalia: "Mallarmé," p. 103.
"Each individual is created for his own sake. The Hebrew metaphysics of individuation is illustrated by the significance of the proper name in the Bible. 'I have known you by your name.' God speaks to Jeremiah as to the particular being that he is: 'before I formed you in the belly I knew you; and before you came forth out of the womb, I sanctified you,' for particular beings are willed and created for their own sake. Each one's name, each one's essence is unique and irreplaceable. Each being is, in the words of Laberthonnière, *apax legomenon.* The metaphysical lesson we may draw from the significance of the proper name is clearly at the counterpole from individuation by matter. It is the seed of Christian personalism" (marginal lining, p. 98).

33 GUARDINI, ROMANO. *The Death of Socrates: An Interpretation of the Platonic Dialogues: Euthyphro, Apology, Crito and Phaedo.* Trans. Basil Wrighton. New York: Sheed and Ward, 1948. 177 + x pp.
Signed, dated 1958.

34 PLATO. *Plato: Apology, Crito, Phaedo, Symposium, Republic.* Trans. B. Jowett. Ed., with an introduction, by Louise Ropes Loomis. Classics Club. New York: Walter J. Black, 1942. 511 + viii pp.

Signed "M. F. O'Connor," dated 1943. Marginal check marks on pp. 258, 264, 274.

Letters, p. 93.

35 ARISTOTLE. *On Man in the Universe: Metaphysics, Parts of Animals, Ethics, Politics, Poetics*. Based on the trans. of John Henry MacMahon, William Ogle, James E. C. Welldon, Benjamin Jowett, and Samuel Henry Butcher. Ed., with an introduction, by Louise Ropes Loomis. Classics Club. New York: Walter J. Black, 1943. 443 + xliii pp.

Signed "M. F. O'Connor," dated 1943.

Letters, pp. 93, 104, 107.

36 GUITTON, JEAN. *The Modernity of Saint Augustine (Actualité de Saint Augustin)*. Trans. A. V. Littledale. Baltimore: Helicon Press, 1959. 89 pp.

Final chapter is also later preface to *Existence et Destinée, le temps et l'éternité chez Plotin et saint Augustin* (Existence and Destiny: Time and Eternity from Plotinus to St. Augustine).

Marginal linings, pp. 13, 15, 16, 24.

Bulletin, 5.14.60; *Reviews*, pp. 90–91.

37 COPLESTON, F. C. *Aquinas*. Pelican Philosophy Series, ed. A. J. Ayer. Harmondsworth, England: Penguin A 349, 1955. 263 pp. Pap.

38 THOMAS AQUINAS, SAINT. *Philosophical Texts*. Selected and trans. Thomas Gilby. New York: Oxford University Press, Galaxy GB 29, 1960 (1951). 405 + xxii pp. Pap.

39 ———. *Truth (Quaestiones Disputatae De veritate)*. Trans. from the definitive Leonine text by Robert W. Mulligan, S.J. Introduction by Vernon J. Bourke. Library of Living Catholic Thought, vol. 1, questions 1–9. Chicago: Henry Regnery, 1952. 472 + xxvi pp.

Signed, dated 1960.

Letters, pp. 107, 367, 368, 370, 499.

40 ———. *Truth (Quaestiones Disputatae De veritate)*. Trans. from the definitive Leonine text by James V. McGlynn, S.J. Library of Living Catholic Thought, vol. 2, questions 10–20. Chicago: Henry Regnery, 1953. 463 + xi pp.

41 ⸻. *Truth (Quaestiones Disputatae De veritate)*. Trans. from the definitive Leonine text by Robert W. Schmidt, S.J. Library of Living Catholic Thought, vol. 3, questions 21–29. Chicago: Henry Regnery, 1954. 530 + xiii pp.

42 JAMES, WILLIAM. *The Selected Letters of William James*. Ed., with an introduction, by Elizabeth Hardwick. Great Letters Series, ed. Louis Kronenberger. New York: Farrar, Straus and Cudahy, 1961. 271 + xxix pp.

43 SANTAYANA, GEORGE. *Persons and Places: The Background of My Life*. [Vol. 1.] New York: Charles Scribner's Sons, 1944. 262 pp. W/o dj.

44 WHITEHEAD, ALFRED NORTH. *Modes of Thought*. New York: Capricorn CAP 5, 1958 (New York, 1938). 241 + viii pp. Pap.

Six lectures delivered at Wellesley College, Massachusetts, and two lectures at the University of Chicago.

45 DE LA BEDOYÈRE, MICHAEL. *The Life of Baron von Hügel*. New York: Charles Scribner's Sons, 1951. 366 + xviii pp. Illus.

Marginal linings on pp. 88, 164, 179.

Letters, pp. 165–67.

46 HÜGEL, BARON FRIEDRICH VON. *Letters from Baron Friedrich von Hügel to a Niece*. Ed., with an introduction, by Gwendolen Greene. Preface by John B. Sheerin, C.S.P. Foreword by Michael La Bedoyère. Thomas More Book to Live. Chicago: Henry Regnery, 1955. 274 pp.

Signed, dated March 1956. O'Connor's note on back of dj: "136." Marginal linings on pp. 23, 33, 36, 39, 41, 51, 65, 68, 71, 121, 122, 127, 135, 153, 154, 159, 171. Underlinings, pp. 40, 64, 65, 83, 84, 94, 105, 113, 121, 123, 136, 159. Question mark, p. 46. Marginalia: "action activity," "zest excitement," p. 159; "HC of CWC," p. 163.

"If there is one danger for religion—if there is any one plausible, all-but-irresistible trend which, throughout its long rich history, has sapped its force, and prepared the most destructive counter-excesses, it is just that—that allowing the fascinations of Grace to deaden or to ignore the beauties and duties of Nature. What *is* Nature? I mean all that, in its degree, is beautiful, true, and good, in this many-leveled world of the one stupendously rich God? Why, Nature (in this sense) is the expression of the God of Nature" (marginal lining, p. 121).

"I mean that religious reading should always be select, slow, ruminating, and given to comparatively few books or papers" (underlined, p. 136).

"Then came Principal Jacks, head of the Unitarian College in Oxford, who, on our subject, 'The Relation between Morals and Religion,' had distressed me, by printing in his paper that a belief in a Beloved Community (= a Church without God) was quite equivalent, as a motive for morality, to faith in God" (marginal notation, p. 163).

> *Bulletin,* 6.23.56; *Reviews,* pp. 21–22; *Letters,* pp. 119, 156, 165, 330–31, 334.

47 COPLESTON, F. C., S.J. *St. Thomas and Nietzsche.* Aquinas Society of London, Aquinas Paper no. 2. London: Blackfriars, 1955 (London, 1944). 24 pp. Pap.

A paper read to the Aquinas Society of London on April 15, 1944.

48 BUBER, MARTIN. *Between Man and Man.* Trans. Ronald Gregor Smith. Humanitas Series. Boston: Beacon Press BP 9, 1955 (Edinburgh, 1947). 211 + vii pp. Pap.

"The five works which I have brought together for English readers in this volume have arisen in connexion with my little book *I and Thou,* as filling out and applying what was said there, with particular regard to the needs of our time" (foreword).

Marginal linings on pp. 14, 15.

49 PASCAL, BLAISE. *Pensées* and *The Provincial Letters.* Trans. W. F. Trotter and Thomas M'Crie, respectively. Introduction by Saxe Commins. Modern Library 164. New York: Random House, 1941. 620 + xvi pp.

> *Letters,* p. 485.

Religion

50 GILSON, ETIENNE. *Reason and Revelation in the Middle Ages.* Scribner Library SL 37. New York: Charles Scribner's Sons, 1938. 114 + vii pp. Pap.
Review unpublished; *Reviews,* p. 129.

51 BUBER, MARTIN. *Eclipse of God: Studies in the Relation between Religion and Philosophy.* New York: Harper and Brothers, Harper Torchbooks TB 12, 1957 (1952). 152 pp. Pap.
On flyleaf: "To Flannery O'Connor from Ted R. Spivey, No. 4, 1958." Marginal linings on pp. 21, 22, 30–31, 33, 35, 68, 73, 97.

"That meaning is open and accessible in the actual lived concrete does not mean it is to be won and possessed through any type of analytical or synthetic investigation or through any type of reflection upon the lived concrete. Meaning is to be experienced in living action and suffering itself, in the unreduced immediacy of the moment" (marginal lining, p. 35).

"I have never in our time encountered on a high philosophical plane such a far-reaching misunderstanding of the prophets of Israel. The prophets of Israel have never announced a God upon whom their hearers' striving for security reckoned. They have always aimed to shatter all security and to proclaim in the opened abyss of the final insecurity the unwished-for God who demands that His human creatures become real, they become human, and confounds all who imagine that they can take refuge in the certainty that the temple of God is in their midst. This is the God of the historical demand as the prophets of Israel beheld Him. The primal reality of these prophecies does not allow itself to be tossed into the attic of 'religions': it is as living and actual in this historical hour as ever" (marginal lining, p. 73).

"The real self appears only when it enters into relation with the Other" (marginal lining, p. 97).

Letters, pp. 302, 303–4.

52 HERBERG, WILL, ED. *Four Existentialist Theologians: A Reader from the Works of Jacques Maritain, Nicholas Berdyaev, Martin Buber and Paul Tillich.* Introduction and biographical notes by Herberg. Garden City, N.Y.: Doubleday, Anchor A141, 1958. 312 + vi pp. Pap.

53 HOSTIE, RAYMOND, S.J. *Religion and the Psychology of Jung.* Trans. G. R. Lamb. New York: Sheed and Ward, 1957. 249 + vi pp.

Signed, dated 1957. Marginal linings on pp. 17, 18, 19, 40, 41, 44, 103, 114, 123, 124, 154, 157, 159, 160, 163, 176, 176–77, 177, 180, 181, 184, 194, 197, 204, 209, 210, 213, 214, 221, 222. Check marks, pp. 125, 212, 220. Correction of text "penitent," p. 164. Marginalia: "Teilhard?" p. 116.

"As consciousness always operates from facts whose content is quite clear, it can never in itself constitute a true symbol. 'An expression that stands for a known thing always remains merely a sign and is never a symbol. It is therefore quite impossible to make a living symbol, i.e., one that is pregnant with meaning, from known associations. For what is thus manufactured never contains more than was put into it" (marginal lining, p. 44).

"I think belief should be replaced by understanding; then we would keep the beauty of the symbol, but still remain free from the depressing results of submission to belief. This would be the psycho-analytic cure for belief and disbelief" (marginal lining, p. 114).

"The dogmatic symbol protects a person from a direct experience of God" (pointed by arrow, p. 136).

"By postulating that good and evil are found together in God Jung believes that he escapes from the dualism that seems inevitable when one stresses the real, positive character of evil as strongly as he does" (pointed by arrow, p. 192).

Review unpublished; *Reviews,* pp. 80–81.

54 STERN, KARL. *The Third Revolution: A Study of Psychiatry and Religion*. New York: Harcourt, Brace, 1954. 306 + vii pp.
  Signed, dated 1955.
  Letters, pp. 91, 103.

55 WHITE, VICTOR, O.P., S.T.B. *God and the Unconscious*. Foreword by C. G. Jung. Appendix by Gebhard Frei. Chicago: Henry Regnery, 1953 (London, 1952). 277 + xxv pp.
  Signed, dated 1954.
  Letters, pp. 103, 382, 451.

56 ———. *God and the Unconscious*. Foreword by C. G. Jung. Appendix by Gebhard Frei. London: Collins, Fontana 463R, 1960 (1952). 287 pp. Pap.

57 ———. *Soul and Psyche: An Enquiry into the Relationship of Psychotherapy and Religion*. New York: Harper and Brothers, 1960. 312 pp.
  Edward Cadbury Lectures, 1958–59.
  Signed, dated 1960. Page numbers noted by O'Connor on dj: "31 61 69 80 167 124 205ff." Marginal linings on pp. 28, 60, 61, 69, 72, 77, 80, 154, 155, 161, 164, 205, 211.

"A mature faith is thus the very opposite of involuntary, unconscious projection. Although it involves a certain courageous surrender of the ego to a mystery which transcends it, the surrender is willed and intended, and by that very fact establishes a relationship to the mystery which excludes unconscious identification with it. Involving lowly obedience, it is a preservative against psychological inflation (*i.e.* identification of the ego with the 'numinous' contents of the unconscious)" (marginal lining, p. 80).

"Evil does exist in things, it is terribly present in them. Evil is real, it actually exists like a wound or mutilation of the being; evil is there in all reality, whenever a thing— which, in so far as it is, and has been, is good—is deprived of some being or of some good it should have" (quoting Maritain; marginal lining, p. 154).

"The whole spectacle of things is that of a procession of

things good wounded by non-being and producing by their activity an indefinitely-increasing accumulation of being and of good, in which that same activity also carries the indefinitely-growing wound—as long as the world exists—of non-being and of evil" (quoting Maritain; marginal lining, p. 155).

> Bulletin, 10.29.60, p.3; *Reviews*, p. 100.

58 ZILBOORG, GREGORY, F.A.P.A. *Freud and Religion: A Restatement of an Old Controversy.* Woodstock Papers, ed. John Courtney Murray, S.J., and Walter J. Burghardt, S.J. Occasional Essays for Theology, no. 3. Westminster, Md.: Newman Press, 1958. 65 + v pp. Pap.

> Marginal linings on pp. 5, 12, 25, 31, 40, 49, 59.

> Bulletin, 1.10.59; *Reviews*, p. 65.

59 BÉGUIN, ALBERT. *Léon Bloy: A Study in Impatience.* Trans. Edith M. Riley. New York: Sheed and Ward, 1947. 247 + vii pp.

> Marginal lining, p. 56.

"It is not Sorrow which grows, it is our sense of it, and this progress is bound up with the imperfection of our minds. That is why we often seem more heroic than we really are. Of our burden we bear only what we see, and we see only part of it. Our Heavenly Father lowers it gradually, sharing the weight between his own hand and our shoulders until habit makes us able to bear the whole pressure without being crushed by it. . . . Through our understanding or our feelings we can never keep pace with the present. That is why sufferings are generally less painful than they may seem; for we bear them by degrees, almost unawares. *Do you know why Jesus Christ has suffered so much?* I will try to give you a transcendent idea of it in a few words. *It is because in his soul, all his lifetime, the present, the past and the future were absolutely one and the same.* This is strikingly true of the Agony in the Garden. But that thought is an abyss . . ." (marginal lining, p. 56).

60 HÜGEL, BARON FRIEDRICH VON. *Essays and Addresses on the*

Philosophy of Religion: First Series. New York: E. P. Dutton, 1949 (Letchworth, 1921). 308 + xix pp.
Signed, dated 1956. Marginal linings on pp. xvi, 6, 11, 13, 23, 47–48, 61, 63, 84, 87, 88, 91, 95, 96, 100, 119, 125, 132, 133, 136, 146, 197, 198, 207, 213, 221, 236, 238, 239 (but crossed out), 240, 267, 268, 269, 280, 288 (triple lined), 292. Underlinings on pp. 13, 14, 33, 48, 60, 61, 62, 87, 88, 94, 96, 104, 125, 246, 263, 266, 267, 268, 269, 292. Check marks on pp. 81, 93, 113, 115, 134, 257. Marginalia: "Raissa Maritain," p. 47; "Art," p. 47; "Rhine," p. 58; "before Tillich?" p. 60; "the Days in Genesis," p. 94; "costingly," p. 104; "Jehova's Witnesses?" p. 138; "Jung vs. White?" p. 214; "the natural now no longer new & strange," p. 246; "& Art," p. 256; "1," p. 257; "2," "3," p. 258; "4," p. 259; "horrible word" (about *Churchmanship*), p. 266; "HW," p. 268; "Hocking," "Haveline," p. 286; "Haveline," p. 291.

"And yet, nothing is more certain than that the richer is any reality, the higher in the scale of being, and the more precious our knowledge of it, the more in part obscure and inexhaustible, the less immediately transferable, is our knowledge of that reality" (marginal lining, p. 11).

"It is by my not denying as false what I do not yet see to be true, that I give myself the chance of growing in insight" (underlined, p. 14).

"The fact is that religion thrives, not by the absence of difficulties, but by the presence of helps and powers; indeed, every step achieved onwards and inwards in such fruitfulness involves new frictions, obscurities, paradoxes, antinomies" (marginal lining, p. 119).

"It is really because of Jesus's utter certainty of the unchanging justice and providence of God that, under the pressure of a proximate earthly defeat of the cause of truth and right, He vividly foresees a corresponding exaltation of this same cause. . . . Jesus would have rejected with horror any and every doctrine of an intrinsically changing, or developing, or even simply successive, God" (marginal lining, p. 133).

"Thus we can only say that even the possibility of sin arises, not from the freedom of the will as such, but, on the contrary, from the imperfection of the freedom; and that there are doubtless reasons, connected with the power of God or with His knowledge (concerning what will, upon the whole, produce a maximum of a certain kind of spiritual happiness), why He chose, or permitted, the existing scheme of imperfect liberty amongst human souls" (marginal lining, p. 221).

Vols. 1 and 2: *Bulletin*, 8.31.57; *Reviews*, pp. 41–42; *Letters*, pp. 165–69, 192, 236, 336.

61 ———. *Essays and Addresses on the Philosophy of Religion: Second Series*. New York: E. P. Dutton, 1951 (1926). 287 pp.

Signed "Flannery O'Connor, Milledgeville, Ga." Marginal linings on pp. 39, 44, 45, 50, 51, 63, 106, 124, 183, 203, 229, 230, 238–39, 248. Underlining on pp. 32, 45, 68, 76, 117, 149, 231, 239, 242. Check mark on p. 265. Marginalia: "see Newman Development of Christian Doctrine: Guitton," p. 18; "see biography by M de Bedoyere," p. 23; "Lewis: *Self-Condemned*," p. 33; "Guitton," p. 50; "Manicheism," p. 71; "fiction: isness," p. 248.

"Next, Professor Rickert points out how that only in proportion as we permit ourselves to be guided by values, by our consciousness of them, do we come to attribute a History, in the strict sense of the word, to some realities and not to others" (underlined, p. 32).

"We cannot, then, accept objective Time otherwise than as a useful convention; and must continuously bear in mind the fact, as certain as it is permanently incomprehensible by our understanding, that the white light of Reality, which fills our consciousness with its real content, is, as it were, broken up and spread out for us, as though by a prism, into a colour-spectrum; so that what, in itself, exists in an immediate unity becomes understandable to us only as a juxtaposition and succession. Beyond that prism there is neither juxtaposition, Space, nor succession, Time" (marginal lining, p. 50).

"Augustine's 'Thou hast made us for Thyself, and our heart is without rest until it rests in Thee,' doubtless requires primarily, to be experienced, God and the human soul; yet it also requires this human soul to be awake to, and to be solicited by, the endless variety of sensible things and of their sensible impressions, furnished by the sensible world" (marginal lining, p. 63).

"And, finally, Religion, in proportion to its religiousness, is everywhere profoundly evidential; it affirms real contacts with a Reality which both occasions and transcends—which exists independently of—all these contacts. Presence, *Isness*, as distinct from the *Oughtness* of Morals: this is the deepest characteristic of all truly religious outlooks. Catholicism is specially concentrated upon this profound Otherness, this Over-against-ness, this *Contrada*, this *Country*, of the Soul. Not the recognition of all the previous requirements of Religion constitutes Catholicism, if the recognition of this final characteristic be lacking" (marginal lining, p. 248).

Vols. 1 and 2: *Bulletin*, 8.31.57; *Reviews*, pp. 41–42.

62 JAMES, WILLIAM. *The Varieties of Religious Experience: A Study in Human Nature*. With a new introduction by Reinhold Niebuhr. New York: Crowell-Collier, Collier AS39, 1961. 416 pp. Pap.

Signed, dated 1963. Marginal linings on pp. 38, 41, 56, 99, 100–101, 104, 139, 140. Check mark, p. 198. Marginalia: "Protestant South + religion aspect," p. 41; "Ho!" p. 241.

"In the Louvre there is a picture, by Guido Reni, of St. Michael with his foot on Satan's neck. The richness of the picture is in large part due to the fiend's figure being there. The richness of its allegorical meaning also is due to his being there—that is, the world is all the richer for having a devil in it, *so long as we keep our foot upon his neck*. In the religious consciousness, that is just the position in which the fiend, the negative or tragic principle, is found" (marginal line, p. 56).

63 KIERKEGAARD, SØREN. *Fear and Trembling* and *The Sickness Unto Death*. Translations, introductions, and notes by Walter Lowrie. Garden City, N.Y.: Doubleday, Anchor A30, 1954 (Princeton, 1941). 278 pp. Pap.

> Marginal lining on p. 174.
>
> *Letters*, p. 273.

64 PICARD, MAX. *The Flight from God*. Trans. Marianne Kuschnitzky and J. M. Cameron. Introduction by Cameron. Humanist Library. Chicago: Henry Regnery, 1951 (Erlenbach, 1934). 185 + xxii pp.

> A note on Max Picard by Gabriel Marcel.
>
> Signed, dated 1952.

65 TEILHARD DE CHARDIN, PIERRE. *The Divine Milieu: An Essay on the Interior Life* (*Le Milieu Divin*). Trans. Bernard Wall. New York: Harper and Brothers, 1960. 144 pp.

> Signed, dated 1960. Marginal lining on p. 102.
>
> "Even children are taught that, throughout the life of each man and the life of the Church and the history of the world, there is only one Mass and one Communion. Christ died once in agony. Peter and Paul receive communion on such and such a day at a particular hour. But these different acts are only the diversely central points in which the continuity of a unique act is split up and fixed, in space and time, for our experience. In fact, from the beginning of the Messianic preparation, up till the Parousia, passing through the historic manifestation of Jesus and the phases of growth of His Church, a single event has been developing in the world: the Incarnation, realised, in each individual, through the Eucharist.
>
> "All the communions of a life-time are one communion.
>
> "All the communions of all men now living are one communion.

"All the communions of all men, present, past and future, are one communion" (marginal lining, p. 102).

Bulletin, 2.4.61; *Reviews*, pp. 107–8; *Letters*, pp. 428, 430, 509, 512.

66 JOURNET, MSGR. CHARLES. *The Wisdom of Faith: An Introduction to Theology*. Trans. R. F. Smith, S.J. Westminster, Md.: Newman Press, 1952. 225 + xvi pp.

67 EBERSOLE, MARK C. *Christian Faith and Man's Religion*. New York: Thomas Y. Crowell, 1961. 206 + x pp.

Marginal lining, p. 9.

Bulletin, 2.17.62; *Reviews*, pp. 135–36.

68 DAWSON, CHRISTOPHER. *Progress and Religion*. Garden City, N.Y.: Doubleday, Image D94, 1960. 200 pp. Pap.

Marginal linings, pp. 22, 32.

"To Hegel the state is the supreme reality which possesses a plentitude and self-sufficiency of being far surpassing that of the individual. It is nothing less than 'the Incarnation of the Divine Idea as it exists on Earth' " (marginal lining, p. 32).

69 BLOY, LÉON. *Pilgrim of the Absolute*. Trans. John Coleman and Harry Lorin Binsse. Selection by Raïssa Maritain. Introduction by Jacques Maritain. New York: Pantheon, 1947. 358 pp.

Signed, dated 1947. Underlining, p. 77.

Letters, p. 130.

70 BROWNSON, ORESTES A. *The Brownson Reader*. Ed., with an introduction, by Alvan S. Ryan. New York: P. J. Kenedy and Sons, 1955.

71 CAPONIGRI, A. ROBERT, ED. *Modern Catholic Thinkers: An Anthology*. Preface by Caponigri. Introduction by Martin Cyril D'Arcy, S.J. New York: Harper and Brothers, 1960. 636 + xvi pp.

Signed, dated 1960. O'Connor's note on front dj: "xv." Marginal linings on pp. 19, 21, 35, 38.

"It is an age-old perplexity, no doubt, but one which,

springing anew with each generation, is felt by each with all its native force. It is the problem of liberty and creed. The life of the Catholic student and scholar is commanded by two principles. There is, on the one hand, the ideal 'sentire cum ecclesia,' to think and feel with the Church, as the basis of his identity as a Catholic; on the other, there is the ideal of free intellectual activity which he shares with every genuine student and scholar, without regard to other commitments and which, he knows, is the sole basis for authentic achievement in the intellectual order. His intention is to realize both in an unbroken harmony which will be reflected both in his person and in his doctrine. Is this intention viable? Or is he, in the nature of the case, engaged in a Quixotic venture, which holds out to him only personal frustration and intellectual sterility?" (passage marked by marginal dot, p. xv).

"The person is absolute, yes, but it is also relative. Is there contradiction here? No, only mystery; the mystery of love which will not be satisfied with the intellectual likeness of its object, but desires it to live as it is in itself and to live with a life which is at the same time the life of one and the life of the other" (marked with an S sign, p. 35).

"But in our struggle and wanderings in search of our one Love and of ourselves we are at the mercy of a disordered imagination, heady passions and unruly impulses, and we are at the mercy of the cunning stranger, the congenial and the novel" (marked with an S sign, p. 38).

Bulletin, 12.24.60; *Reviews*, pp. 103–4.

72 MAURIAC, FRANÇOIS. *Words of Faith* (*Paroles Catholiques*). Trans. Rev. Edward H. Flannery. New York: Philosophical Library, 1955. 118 pp.

73 ROUGEMONT, DENIS DE. *The Christian Opportunity*. Trans. Donald Lehmkuhl. New York: Holt, Rinehart and Winston, 1963. 185 + xiii pp.

Signed, dated 1964. Marginal markings on pp. 18, 19, 20,

23, 27, 28. Marginal linings on pp. 64, 114, 116. Underlining on p. 84.

"Sincerity has scarcely any significance in art" (underlined, p. 84).

Review unpublished; *Reviews*, pp. 168–69.

74 STEIN, EDITH. *Writings of Edith Stein*. Selected and trans., with an introduction, by Hilda Graef. Westminster, Md.: Newman Press, 1956. 206 pp.

Marginal linings, pp. 22, 39, 41, 43. Underlinings on pp. 77, 78. Check marks, pp. 38, 39. Marginalia: "experiential?" p. 84.

"symbolic language. . . . will also induce knowledge of something not yet known" (underlined, p. 77).

Bulletin, 3.2.57; *Reviews*, pp. 34–35; *Letters*, p. 207.

75 WEIGEL, GUSTAVE, S.J. *The Modern God: Faith in a Secular Culture*. New York: Macmillan, 1963. 168 + v pp.

O'Connor's numbers on dj: "8, 17, 27, 31, 37, 63, 98, 107/185, 168." Marginal check marks on pp. 15, 27, 31, 32, 33, 37, 63, 98, 107.

"If the gospel is to be preached to every creature, the gospel must be expressed in the media of the creatures to be evangelized" (checked on p. 107).

Bulletin, 9.26.63; *Reviews*, pp. 162–63.

76 LEPP, IGNACE. *Atheism in Our Time* (*Psychoanalyse de l'atheisme moderne*). Trans. Bernard Murchland, C.S.C. New York: Macmillan, 1963. 195 pp.

Signed on half-title page, dated 1963.

77 LUBAC, HENRI DE, S.J. *The Drama of Atheist Humanism*. Trans. Edith M. Riley. Cleveland: World Publishing, Meridian M165, 1963 (New York, 1950). 253 + ix pp. Pap. Illus.

Signed, dated 1963. O'Connor has checked three titles in the catalog at the back of the book: Lord Acton, *Lectures on Modern History*; Perry Miller, *Jonathan Edwards*; Nicholas Berdyaev, *Dostoevsky*.

78 KELLY, BERNARD. *The Metaphysical Background of Analogy*.

Aquinas Society of London, Aquinas Paper no. 29. London: Blackfriars, 1958. 23 pp. Pap.

A paper read to the Aquinas Society of London in 1957.

79 MALEVEZ, L., S.J. *The Christian Message and Myth: The Theology of Rudolf Bultmann.* Trans. Olive Wyon. Westminster, Md.: Newman Press, 1958; *Le Message Chrétien et le Mythe* (Brussels, 1954). 215 pp.

Signed, dated April 1960. Marginal linings, pp. 44, 54, 58, 59, 60, 61, 68, 75, 77, 78, 79, 104, 108, 115, 116, 117, 119, 125, 126–27, 128, 130, 141. Underlining on p. 79. Check marks, pp. 124, 167, 178, 181, 183, 205. Marginalia: "Name them?" bottom of p. 36.

Bulletin, 7.23.60; *Reviews*, p. 92.

80 THE FURROW. *The Word of Life: Essays on the Bible.* Foreword by E. J. Kissane. Westminster, Md.: Newman Press, 1960. 123 + viii pp. Pap.

"The essays contained in this book first appeared in *The Furrow* during 1957. They are published here with the permission of the Editor for the Furrow Trust."

Flyleaf signed "Sister Julia to Flannery O'Connor"; half-title page signed "Sister Julia." Marginal lining on p. 9. Check mark on p. 51.

81 MCKENZIE, JOHN L., S.J., ED. *The Bible in Current Catholic Thought.* Saint Marys Theology Studies, no. 1. New York: Herder and Herder, 1962. 247 + xiii pp. Illus.

Signed, dated 1963.

82 WOODS, RALPH L., ED. *The Catholic Companion to the Bible.* Foreword by the Most Reverend John J. Wright. Philadelphia: J. B. Lippincott, 1956. 313 pp.

An anthology of Catholic writing on the Bible from St. Jerome to Jacques Maritain.

Signed, dated 1956. Marginal lining, pp. 165, 203. Check mark, p. 164. Marginalia: "von Hugel," p. 165.

"Thus in the prophetic writings we find allegory, parable, symbolic images, strange dramatic actions described, all bearing a marked individuality of style and thought" (check mark, p. 164).

> *Bulletin*, 9.1.56; *Reviews*, pp. 25–26.

83 BURNS, J. EDGAR, S.T.D., S.S.L. *Hear His Voice Today: A Guide to the Content and Comprehension of the Bible.* New York: P. J. Kenedy and Sons, 1963. 207 + ix pp.

> "172" noted by O'Connor on back dj. Marginal lining on p. 172.

84 ALONSO SCHÖKEL, LUIS, S.J. *Understanding Biblical Research* (*El Hombre de Hoy Ante la Biblia*). Trans. Peter J. McCord, S.J. Foreword by Joseph A. Fitzmyer, S.J. New York: Herder and Herder, 1963. 130 + xii pp.

> Signed, dated 1963. Marginal linings on pp. 33, 90. Check marks on pp. 35, 39.

85 GUILLET, JACQUES. *Themes of the Bible.* Trans. Albert J. La-Mothe, Jr. Notre Dame, Ind.: Fides Publishers, 1960; *Thèmes Bibliques* (Paris, 1954). 279 pp.

> *Bulletin*, 9.16.61; *Reviews*, p. 121.

86 LEVIE, JEAN, S.J. *The Bible, Word of God in Words of Men.* Trans. S. H. Treman. New York: P. J. Kenedy and Sons, 1961; *La Bible, Parole Humaine et Message de Dieu* (Paris-Louvain, 1958). 323 + x pp. W/o dj.

> Marginal linings on pp. viii, ix, 15, 23, 25, 26, 34, 53, 54, 68, 77, 214, 219. Underlinings on pp. 15, 215, 216. Check marks on pp. 210, 211, 212, 215.
>
> *Southern Cross*, 3.2.63; *Reviews*, pp. 155–56.

87 BIBLE. *The Kingdom of God: A Short Bible.* Translations, explanations, and paraphrases under the direction of Louis J. Putz, C.S.C. Notre Dame, Ind.: Fides Publishers, 1962; *Reich Gottes* (Munich, 1960). 383 pp. Illus. Maps. Plasticine wrap.

> Signed, dated 1962.
>
> *Southern Cross*, 1.9.64.

88 BIBLE. *The Holy Bible: Douay Version.* Trans. from the Latin Vulgate. Preface by the Cardinal Archbishop of Westminster. Notes compiled by Bishop Challoner (1691–1781).

London: Catholic Truth Society, 1957 (London, 1956). 1,282 + 349 pp.

"The preparation of this edition of the Bible has provided the opportunity to make, with the sanction of Authority, certain emendations, mainly of a grammatical nature, to the current Douay texts. Footnotes have been added where these emendations occur in the text."

Signed, dated 1959. Marginal notations to Genesis 4:21; 15:12; 28:12; 31:11, 12, 24, 47; 37:6, 9, 19; Numbers 12:5–9; Judith 9:4–6. Paperclip marking Matthew 11. Noted by O'Connor on dj: "No. 12:8."

89 POELMAN, ROGER. *Times of Grace: The Sign of Forty in the Bible.* Trans. D. P. Farina. Preface by John L. McKenzie. New York: Herder and Herder, 1964; *Le signe biblique des quarante jours* (Paris, 1961). 189 pp.

90 ROWLEY, H. H. ED. *The Old Testament and Modern Study: A Generation of Discovery and Research.* London: Oxford University Press, Oxford Paperbacks 18, 1961 (Oxford, 1951). 405 + xxxi pp. Pap.

Essays by members of the Society for Old Testament Study.

Marginal lining on p. 25.

Bulletin, 12.9.61; *Reviews*, pp. 125–26.

91 BIBLE. *The Old Testament.* Newly trans. from Latin Vulgate by Msgr. Ronald Knox. Vol. 1, *Genesis to Esther.* New York: Sheed and Ward, 1948. 739 pp.

Translated at the request of the Cardinal Archbishop of Westminster.

Signed, dated 1949. Marginal lining for 3 Kings 19:11–14.

92 ———. *The Old Testament.* Newly trans. from Latin Vulgate by Msgr. Ronald Knox. Vol. 2, *Job to Machabees.* New York: Sheed and Ward, 1950. 863 + vi pp. (pp. 741–1,604).

Translated at the request of the Cardinal Archbishop of Westminster. Appendix (alternative version of Psalms).

Marginal lining at Isaias 13:21–22.

93 GELIN, ALBERT. *The Key Concepts of the Old Testament (Les Idées Maîtresses de l'Ancien Testament).* Trans. George Lamb. New York: Sheed and Ward, 1955. 94 + xiv pp.

94 JONES, ALEXANDER, S.T.L., L.S.S. *Unless Some Man Show Me.* New York: Paulist Press, Deus Books, 1962 (New York, 1951). 160 pp. Pap.
Signed, dated 1962.

95 WRIGHT, G. ERNEST, ED. *The Bible and the Ancient Near East.* Garden City, N.Y.: Doubleday, 1961. 409 pp.
Essays in honor of William Foxwell Albright.
Marginal lining for "Yemen" in subject index, p. 409.
Bulletin, 12.9.61; *Reviews,* pp. 125–26.

96 McKENZIE, JOHN L., S.J. *The Two-Edged Sword: An Interpretation of the Old Testament.* Milwaukee: Bruce Publishing, 1956. 317 + xv pp.
Signed, dated December 1956. Marginal lining on p. 156.
"That is what the writers of the codes of law and of the prophets mean when they speak of national sin. Sin, to them, is not merely a moral disorder, a breach of a statute; it is a cosmic disorder, with repercussions that go far beyond the moral order and affect the entire life of man—his biological, social, political, economic welfare. For all these things depend upon the maintenance of the cosmic harmony of man submitted to the will of the Lord; once this harmony is disturbed, the harmony of the whole is lost. This is the Hebrew belief" (marginal lining, p. 156).
Bulletin, 1.9.57; *Reviews,* pp. 33–34; *Letters,* p. 237.

97 CHAINE, J. *God's Heralds: A Guide to the Prophets of Israel.* Trans. Brendan McGrath, O.S.B. New York: Joseph F. Wagner, 1955; *Introduction à la lecture des Prophètes* (Paris, 1946). 236 + xiv pp. Maps.
Marginal lining, p. 123. Underlining on p. 157. O'Connor's note on dj: "123 swallow the book 157." Textual correction, p. 153.
"Face to face with the grandeur of Yahweh, Ezechiel is a

'son of man,' a weak being, a member of humanity, a creature of no account. God established him as a prophet in the
midst of his brethren, who are compared to thorns and scor-
pions. Ezechiel receives an order to swallow a book full of
lamentations in order that he may assimilate and then utter
them to the children of Juda. In the Apocalypse (10:1–11) St.
John also swallows a book. In the Orient there was an ancient
custom of swallowing a book as a means of assimilating its
power. Isaias (6:8) offers himself to God at the moment of his
call, whereas Jeremias (1:6) seeks to excuse himself: Ezechiel
meditates in his soul on the bitterness and wrath. Like Jeremias (20:7–9), he feels himself subdued by grace, as God's
hand makes its might felt in him (3:14). God next makes him
understand how terrible his responsibility is (3:16–21). It was
from this moment that Ezechiel took up his work as a senti-
nel in the midst of the captives" (marginal lining, p. 123).

    Bulletin, 8.3.57; *Reviews,* p. 41.

98 VAWTER, BRUCE, C. M. *A Path through Genesis.* New York:
Sheed and Ward, 1956. 308 + ix pp. Illus. Maps.

    Signed, dated October, 1956. O'Connor's notation on dj:
"34 35 49." Marginal linings on pp. 34, 35, 49. Underlining
on p. 36.

    "Fundamentalism is not born of respect for the Bible. It is
born of contempt for man's God-given intellect. It has failed
the most elementary task of religion, which is the rational
service of God" (underlining, p. 36).

    Bulletin, 1.19.57; *Reviews,* pp. 32–33; *Letters,* p. 237.

99 AUGUSTINE. *Nine Sermons of Saint Augustine on the Psalms.*
Trans., with an introduction, by Edmund Hill, O.P., S.T.L.
New York: P. J. Kenedy and Sons, 1959. [177] + xi pp.

    Signed, dated 1959. Marginal linings on pp. 38, 65. Un-
derlining on p. 67. Check mark (for "hangover") on p. 63.
Question mark, p. 62. Marginalia: questioned "inside information," p. 52, and "postman," p. 53; wrote "ugh" next to
"Got it?" p. 66.

"Now let us look at the psalm [25] a little more closely. For you see, when a man makes progress in the life of the Church, he has to suffer much from bad people in the Church. There's simply no avoiding it. He does indeed try not to notice them, even though bad people are for ever complaining bitterly about each other; after all, it is easier for one man in good health to put up with two invalids than it is for them to put up with each other. Still I want to warn you about this, brothers; the Church in this world is a threshing-floor, and as I have often said before and still say now, it is piled high with chaff and grain together. It is no use trying to be rid of all the chaff before the time comes for winnowing" (marginal lining, p. 65).

Bulletin, 7.25.54; *Reviews*, p. 74; *Letters*, p. 330.

100 VAWTER, BRUCE, C.M. *The Conscience of Israel: Pre-exilic Prophets and Prophecy*. New York: Sheed and Ward, 1961. 308 + xii pp. Maps.

Signed, dated 1961. Marginal linings on pp. 5, 6, 7, 14, 16, 17, 30, 34, 38, 40, 152. Underlining on p. 6. Check mark on p. 39.

"We must see them for what they considered themselves to be and were, devoted Israelites, believers in the destiny of their people, looking for a regeneration of Israel that it might continue to be what Yahweh had planned for it. We have not yet taken in their words until we have reset them—to the extent that this is possible for us—in the concrete historical moment that provoked them into being. When their words remain obscure for us, often as not this means that we have been unable to recreate this historical moment" (marginal lining, p. 7).

Bulletin, 3.17.62, p. 6; *Reviews*, p. 141.

101 BRILLET, GASTON, C. OR. *Meditations on the Old Testament*. Vol. 3, *Prophecy*. Trans. Jane Wynne Saul, R.S.C.J. New York: Desclee, 1961; *365 Méditations sur la Bible—La Prophétie* (Paris, 1958). 274 pp.

102 Van Zeller, Dom Hubert. *The Outspoken Ones: Twelve Prophets of Israel and Juda.* New York: Sheed and Ward, 1955. 195 + xx pp. Map.

103 Bible. *The New Testament of Our Lord and Saviour Jesus Christ.* Trans. R. A. Knox. New York: Sheed and Ward, 1948. 573 pp. W/o dj.

A new translation at the request of the Hierarchy of England and Wales.

Signed, dated 1949. Marginal linings at John 15:22–23; 1 Corinthians 3:16–18. Marginal check mark at Matthew 5:3.

"Do you not understand that you are God's temple, and that God's Spirit has his dwelling in you? If anybody desecrates the temple of God, God will bring him to ruin. It is a holy thing, this temple of God which is nothing other than yourselves. You must not deceive yourselves, any of you, about this" (1 Corinthians 3:16–18, marginal lining on p. 345).

104 Toal, M. F., ed. *Patristic Homilies on the Gospels.* Vol. 1, *From the First Sunday of Advent to Quinquagesima.* Trans. M. F. Toal. Chicago: Henry Regnery, 1955. 503 pp. W/o dj.

105 Knox, Ronald. *St. Paul's Gospel.* New York: Sheed and Ward, 1951. 72 pp.

"This series of Lenten Conferences was preached by Msgr. Ronald Knox in Westminster Cathedral on the Sunday evenings in Lent, 1950."

106 Daniélou, Jean. *The Dead Sea Scrolls and Primitive Christianity (Les Manuscrits de la Mer Morte et les origines du Christianisme).* Trans. Salvator Attanasio. New York: New American Library, Mentor Omega MP 405, 1962 (1958). 128 + ix pp. Photographs. Pap.

Letters, p. 298.

107 Callahan, Daniel J., Heiko A. Oberman, and Daniel J. O'Hanlon, S.J., eds. *Christianity Divided: Protestant and Roman Catholic Theological Issues.* New York: Sheed and Ward, 1961. 335 + xiv pp.

Bulletin, 2.17.62; *Reviews,* pp. 135–36.

108 LEWIS, C. S. *The Case for Christianity.* New York: Macmillan, 1944. 56 pp. W/o dj.

Published in England as "Broadcast Talks."

O'Connor has pasted in a color photograph of Lewis from a magazine opposite the title page. Signed "M. F. O'Connor, Milledgeville, Ga."

109 WATTS, ALAN W. *Myth and Ritual in Christianity.* New York: Grove Press, Evergreen E-212, 1960 (New York, 1954). 262 + [ix] pp. Illus. Pap.

Letters, p. 451.

110 ULANOV, BARRY. *Sources and Resources: The Literary Tradition of Christian Humanism.* Westminster, Md.: Newman Press, 1960. 286 + xv pp.

111 NEWMAN, JOHN HENRY CARDINAL. *An Essay on the Development of Christian Doctrine.* Ed. Charles Frederick Harrold. New York: Longmans, Green, 1949. 456 + xl pp.

New edition with a preface and introduction by Harrold. An appendix on Newman's textual changes by Ottis Ivan Schreiber.

Signed, dated 1949.

112 GUARDINI, ROMANO. *The Faith and Modern Man* (*Glaubenserkenntnis*). Trans. Charlotte E. Forsyth. New York: Pantheon, 1952. 166 + vii pp.

Letters, pp. 133–34.

113 NEWMAN, JOHN HENRY CARDINAL. *An Essay in Aid of a Grammar of Assent.* Introduction by Etienne Gilson. Garden City, N.Y.: Doubleday, Image D19, 1955. 396 pp. Pap.

Marginal linings on pp. 10, 63, 65, 87, 89. Underlinings on pp. 55, 59, 63, 65.

"Words which make nonsense, do not make a mystery" (underlined, p. 55).

"Belief, on the other hand, being concerned with things concrete, not abstract, which variously excite the mind from their moral and imaginative properties, has for its objects, not only directly what is true, but inclusively what is beautiful, useful, admirable, heroic; objects which kindle devotion, rouse the passions, and attach the affections" (marginal lining, p. 87).

"The heart is commonly reached, not through the reason, but through the imagination, by means of direct impressions, by the testimony of facts and events, by history, by description. Persons influence us, voices melt us, looks subdue us, deeds inflame us. Many a man will live and die upon a dogma; no man will be a martyr for a conclusion. A conclusion is but an opinion; it is not a thing which *is*, but which we are *'quite sure about'*; and it has often been observed, that we never say we are sure and certain without implying that we doubt. To say that a thing *must* be, is to admit that it *may not* be. No one, I say, will die for his own calculations: he dies for realities. This is why a literary religion is so little to be depended upon; it looks well in fair weather; but its doctrines are opinions, and, when called to suffer for them, it slips them between its folios, or burns them at its hearth" (marginal lining, p. 89).

Letters, p. 477.

114 TAVARD, GEORGE H., A.A. *Transiency and Permanence: The Nature of Theology According to St. Bonaventure.* Franciscan Institute Publications Theology Series no. 4, ed. Eligius M. Buytaert, O.F.M. St. Bonaventure, N.Y.: Franciscan Institute, 1954. 263 + vii pp. Pap.

Marginal linings on pp. 62, 63, 65, 66. Underlining on p. 63.

"As far as the exterior world is concerned, knowledge starts from sense activity. Given the finality of the material world, senses are needed for the interior harmony of man, a spiritual creature destined to assume material objects in his ascent to God. The passage of human knowledge confers upon sense a spiritual value. Far from being left behind by the detection of likenesses of God in created beings, the Book of Nature, urging man to further research of God, reached its own finality. With such an end, sense percep-

tion must be continued by intellectual knowledge. In connexion with this, it is relevant to wonder whether the reading of signs of God in the objects of knowledge is incipient
with sensation itself or waits until the intellectual plane is
reached.

"An answer to this question is important enough for a
right appreciation of St. Bonaventure's view on the Book of
Nature. In the hypothesis that sensation has a positive role
in deciphering the signs of God—if, in other words, a de-
part between true and false knowledge originates in a cleavage in the structure of sense activity—we normally ought to
conclude that sense forms the first degree of the way to God
and has thus a momentous religious value. A re-valorisa-
tion of man's bodily senses would then follow" (marginal
lining, p. 62).

"There is a Bonaventurian thesis according to which any
act of knowledge is compounded of two movements, called
'reception' and 'judgment.' 'Reception' is the contacting of
an object by the senses. 'Judgment' is the active acceptance
of that contact" (marginal lining, p. 63; last sentence also
underlined).

"From the theological tradition St. Bonaventure received
the Augustinian principle that the Word is the Sun of the
mind, the light thanks to which created spirits are able to
see intellectually" (marginal lining, p. 66).

     Letters, pp. 189, 227, 228, 229.

115   TEACHING. *The Teaching of the Catholic Church: A Summary of
Catholic Doctrine.* Ed. Canon George D. Smith. Vol. 1. New
York: Macmillan, 1949 (New York, 1927). 658 + xiv pp.

     Entries 115 and 116 are a boxed set.

     Signed, dated 1949.

116   ———. *The Teaching of the Catholic Church: A Summary of
Catholic Doctrine.* Ed. Canon George D. Smith. Vol. 2. New
York: Macmillan, 1949 (New York, 1927). 657 + xiii pp. (pp.
659–1,316).

117 BARTH, KARL. *Evangelical Theology: An Introduction (Einführung in die evangelische Theologie)*. Trans. Grover Foley. New York: Holt, Rinehart and Winston, 1963. 206 + xiii pp.

"The first five lectures of this volume were delivered under the auspices of the Divinity School, the University of Chicago, and were 'The Annie Kinkead Warfield Lectures of 1962' at the Princeton Theological Seminary."

Signed, dated 1963. Marginal linings on pp. 9, 11, 18, 23, 24, 31–32, 39, 39–40, 45, 48, 49, 55, 64, 65, 70, 86, 91, 94, 104, 113, 118, 119, 136, 138, 151–52, 152 (double lines). Underlining on p. 97. Check marks on pp. 5, 6, 7, 15, 21, 30, 31, 71, 73, 75, 89, 177. Marginalia: "St. Thomas: 'all straw,' " p. 137.

"He is the God who again and again discloses himself anew and must be discovered anew" (checked, p. 6).

"Evangelical theology is *modest* theology, because it is determined to be so by its object, that is, by him who is its subject" (checked, p. 7).

"A quite specific *astonishment* stands at the beginning of every theological perception, inquiry, and thought, in fact at the root of every theological word. This astonishment is indispensable if theology is to exist and be perpetually renewed as a modest, free, critical, and happy science" (marginal lining, p. 64).

" 'I hear the message well enough, but what I lack is faith,' said Goethe's Faust. Yes, indeed—who does *not* lack faith? Who *can* believe? Certainly no one would believe if he maintained that he 'had' faith, so that nothing was lacking to him, and that he 'could' believe. Whoever believes, knows and confesses that he cannot 'by his own understanding and power' in any way believe. He will simply *perform* this believing, without losing sight of the unbelief that continually accompanies him and makes itself felt. Called and illumined by the Holy Spirit as he is, he does not understand himself; he cannot help but completely wonder at himself" (marginal lining, p. 104).

"It is a terrible thing when God keeps silence, and by keeping silence speaks" (marginal lining, p. 136).

"The God of whom we speak is no god imagined or devised by men. The grace of the gods who are imagined or devised by men is usually a conditional grace, to be merited and won by men through supposedly good works, and not the true grace which gives itself freely. Instead of being hidden under the form of a contradiction, *sub contrario,* and directed to man through radical endangering and judgment, man's imagined grace is usually directly offered and accessible in some way to him and can be rather conveniently, cheaply, and easily appropriated. Evangelical theology, on the other hand, is to be pursued in hope, though as a human work it is radically questioned by God, found guilty in God's judgment and verdict—and though collapsing long before it reaches its goal, it relies on God who himself seeks out, heals, and saves man and his work. This God is the hope of theology" (double marginal lining, p. 152).

Southern Cross, 10.24.63; *Reviews,* pp. 164–65; *Letters,* pp. 306, 523, 525.

118 TRESMONTANT, CLAUDE. *Toward the Knowledge of God.* Trans. Robert J. Olsen. Baltimore: Helicon Press, 1961; *Essai sur la Connaissance de Dieu* (Paris, 1959). 120 + vii pp.

Signed "Flannery O'Connor, Milledgeville, Ga., 1961." Marginal linings on pp. 3, 12, 24, 79, 84, 88–89. Check marks on pp. 25, 26, 82, 83.

"Nor is the world as a whole any more divine than any of its elements. This is a repudiation of idolatry and consequently of fetishism; it is a denunciation of astrolatry, totemism, emperor-worship, etc. This cathartic critique is the necessary, negative preparation for the coming of positive knowledge" (passage marked by check mark, p. 82).

"He [God] will not tolerate our wallowing in the emptiness of idolatry, the worship of those images which our hands have fashioned or our thoughts have conceived. He will not allow us to return to nothingness. The wrath of God is actually the love of God, intolerant of vanity, injustice, the crime of man against man, and against Himself. How badly the Bible has been read if we believe that the God of the Old Testament is a God of wrath and strictness, quite devoid of love! And how badly the New Testament has been read if we have not found on every page something of the wrath of God and the warning of God! In both testaments the same wrath and the same love are expressed, the same wrath expressing the same love" (marginal lining, pp. 88–89).

    Bulletin, 5.12.62.

119 D'ARCY, M. C., S.J. *The Mind and Heart of Love: Lion and Unicorn, A Study in Eros and Agape*. New York: Henry Holt, 1947. 333 pp. W/o dj.

    Signed, dated 1947. Marginal linings on pp. 51, 65. Underlinings on pp. 51, 215.

120 LOVE. *Love and Violence (Amour et Violence)*. Ed. Père Bruno de Jésus-Marie, O.C.D. Trans. George Lamb. New York: Sheed and Ward, 1954 (1946). 260 + ix pp. Illus.

121 CRANSTON, RUTH. *The Miracle of Lourdes*. New York: Popular Library, Giant G199, 1957 (New York, 1955). 251 pp. Pap.

122 ADAM, KARL. *The Christ of Faith: The Christology of the Church*. Trans. Joyce Crick. New York: Pantheon, 1957; *Der Christus des Glaubens* (Düsseldorf, n.d.). 364 + x pp.

    Marking, p. 5.

    Bulletin, 4.5.58; *Reviews*, pp. 54–55; *Letters*, pp. 231, 244, 296, 449.

123 CHURCH. *The Church as the Body of Christ*. Studies and Research in Christian Theology at Notre Dame, vol. 1, by K. E. Skydsgaard; Barnabas Ahern, C.P.; Walter J. Burghardt, S.J.; Bernard Cooke, S.J.; and Dr. Franklin H. Littell. Cardinal O'Hara Series, ed. Robert S. Pelton. Notre Dame, Ind.: University of Notre Dame Press, 1963. 145 + xii pp. W/o dj.

    Marginal lining on p. 51. Check mark on p. 52.

124 MAURIAC, FRANÇOIS. *The Son of Man*. Trans. Bernard Murchland. Cleveland: World Publishing, 1960; *Le Fils de l'homme* (Paris, 1958). 158 pp.
Marginal lining on p. 39.
Bulletin, 9.3.60, p. 7; *Reviews*, pp. 95–96.

125 GUARDINI, ROMANO. *Jesus Christus: Meditations*. Trans. Peter White. Chicago: Henry Regnery, 1959; *Jesus Christus, Geistliches Wort* (Würzburg, 1957). 111 pp.
Marginalia: "th?" p. 46.
Bulletin, 2.6.60, p. 5; *Reviews*, p. 85.

126 ADAM, KARL. *The Son of God*. Trans. Philip Hereford. Garden City, N.Y.: Doubleday, Image D99, 1960 (New York, 1934). 235 pp. Pap.
Letters, p. 369.

127 DANIEL-ROPS, HENRI. *Jesus and His Times*. Trans. Ruby Millar. New York: E. P. Dutton, 1954. 615 pp.

128 GUARDINI, ROMANO. *The Lord*. Trans. Elinor Castendyk Briefs. Chicago: Henry Regnery, 1954. 535 + xi pp.
Signed, dated 1954.
Letters, pp. 74, 99, 106, 169, 296.

129 WEIGER, JOSEF. *Mary, Mother of Faith*. Trans. Ruth Mary Bethell. Introduction to the English translation by Msgr. Romano Guardini. Chicago: Henry Regnery, 1959; *Maria die Mutter des Glaubens* (Aschaffenburg, n.d.). [260] + xi pp.
Bulletin, 2.6.60, p. 5; *Reviews*, p. 85.

130 DURRWELL, F. X., C.S.R. *The Resurrection: A Biblical Study (La Résurrection de Jésus, mystère de salut)*. Trans. Rosemary Sheed. Introduction by Charles Davis, S.T.L. New York: Sheed and Ward, 1960. 371 + xxvi pp.
Bulletin, 9.16.61; *Reviews*, p. 120.

131 ALTER, THE MOST REV. KARL J. *The Mind of an Archbishop: A Study of Man's Essential Relationship to God, Church, Country, and Fellow Man*. Ed. Rev. Maurice E. Reardon, S.T.D. Foreword by the Most Rev. Paul F. Leibold, J.C.D. Cincinnati: Archdiocese of Cincinnati, 1960. 406 + xix pp. W/o dj.
Golden Jubilee edition.

132 GUARDINI, ROMANO. *Freedom, Grace, and Destiny: Three Chapters in the Interpretation of Existence* (*Freiheit, Gnade, Schicksal*). Trans. John Murray, S.J. New York: Pantheon, 1961. 251 pp.

Marginal linings on pp. 10, 28, 37, 44, 72, 80, 81. Underlining on p. 10.

"In general, the answer is that the free act derives its full validity from the fact that it is not just any kind of act but the right act" (marginal lining, p. 28).

"Modern ethics argues that when man obeys God's commandments he becomes heteronomous, belonging to someone outside himself, whereas freedom fundamentally consists in autonomy, in perfect self-dependence. But this argument understands freedom as absolute freedom and thus equates human freedom with Divine freedom. Were that the case, obedience to God would certainly take away human liberty. But in fact, God alone is God; man, conversely, is His creature. Man's freedom is a created freedom and it therefore develops essentially before God and in subordination to Him" (marginal lining, p. 81).

Bulletin, 10.28.61; *Reviews*, p. 123.

133 VANN, GERALD, O.P. *The Heart of Man.* Garden City, N.Y.: Doubleday, Image D103, 1960 (New York, 1945). 190 pp. Pap.

134 CONGAR, YVES, O.P. *The Wide World My Parish: Salvation and Its Problems* (*Vaste Monde, ma Paroisse*). Trans. Donald Attwater. Baltimore: Helicon Press, [1961]. 188 + xi pp.

Signed, dated 1962. Marginal linings on pp. 96, 97.

Southern Cross, 3.23.63, p. 7; *Reviews*, p. 159.

135 TERESA OF JESUS, SAINT. *The Interior Castle or The Mansions.* Trans. a Discalced Carmelite. Westminster, Md.: Newman Bookshop, [1945]. 122 + vi pp. W/o dj.

Signed, dated 1949.

Letters, p. 166.

136 JOURNET, CHARLES. *The Meaning of Grace.* Trans. A. V. Littledale. New York: P. J. Kenedy and Sons, 1960; *Entretiens sur la Grâce* (n.p., 1959). 127 + xii pp.

Signed, dated 1960. Marginal notation on p. 35.

Bulletin, 7.22.61; *Reviews,* p. 118.

137 PIEPER, JOSEF. *Belief and Faith: A Philosophical Tract.* Trans. Richard Winston and Clara Winston. New York: Pantheon, 1963; *Über den Glauben* (n.p., 1962). 106 + [xii] pp.

Signed, dated 1963. O'Connor's numbers on dj: "6 8 20 23 55 61 62 72 88." Marginal linings on pp. 65, 72, 88. Check marks on pp. 55, 61, 62, 63, 73.

"Unbelief in the precise sense of the term is only that mental act in which someone deliberately refuses assent to a truth which he has recognized with sufficient plainness to be God's speech" (marginal lining, p. 72).

138 HEANEY, JOHN J., S.J., ED. *Faith, Reason, and the Gospels: A Selection of Modern Thought on Faith and the Gospels.* Westminster, Md.: Newman Press, 1962. 327 + xiii pp.

Check marks on pp. 179, 217.

"For Herr Bultmann, salvation is not the event of the year 30, but a change in man's understanding of himself" (check mark, p. 179).

Southern Cross, 7.18.63; *Catholic Week,* 11.27.63, p. 7; *Reviews,* pp. 166–67.

139 BRUNO, FATHER DE, J.M., O.D.C., ED. *Three Mystics: El Greco, St. John of the Cross, St. Teresa of Avila.* New York: Sheed and Ward, 1949. 187 pp. Illus.

Letters, p. 189.

140 [BUTLER, REV. ALBAN. *The Lives of the Fathers, Martyrs, and Other Principal Saints.* Vol. 1. Baltimore: Metropolitan Press, 1845.] 428 + xl pp. W/o dj.

"Compiled from Original Monuments and other Authentic Records, Illustrated with the Remarks of Judicious Modern Critics and Historians." Title page missing. Heavily foxed.

141 ———. *The Lives of the Fathers, Martyrs, and Other Principal Saints.* Vol. 2. Baltimore: Metropolitan Press, 1845. 484 pp. W/o dj.

Heavily foxed. Flyleaf signed "Treanor of Milledgeville Georgia."

142 ———. *The Lives of the Fathers, Martyrs, and Other Principal Saints.* Vol. 3. Baltimore: Metropolitan Press, 1845. [566] pp. W/o dj.

Heavily foxed. Spine partly missing. Flyleaf signed "Treanor of Milledgeville Georgia."

143 ———. *The Lives of the Fathers, Martyrs, and Other Principal Saints.* Vol. 4. Baltimore: Metropolitan Press, 1845. 598 + 52 + [20] pp. W/o dj.

Heavily foxed. Spine partly missing. Flyleaf signed "Treanor of Milledgeville, Georgia."

144 CONYNGHAM, D. P. *Lives of the Irish Saints: From St. Patrick down to St. Laurence O'Toole.* Introduction by Rev. Thomas S. Preston. New York: D. and J. Sadlier, 1870. 576 + xxiv pp. Illus.

O'Connor's note on inside back cover: "Errors: 51 107 109 114?" and "71." Marginalia (probably not hers) on pp. 29, 51, 321.

145 SCHAMONI, WILHELM. *The Face of the Saints.* Trans. Anne Fremantle. New York: Pantheon, 1947. [279] pp. Photographs. W/o dj.

Signed.

146 GUARDINI, ROMANO. *The Conversion of Augustine.* Trans. Elinor Briefs. Westminster, Md.: Newman Press, 1960; *Die Bekehrung des Aurelius Augustinus* (Munich, n.d.). 258 + xviii pp.

A selection of the Catholic Book Club.

O'Connor has noted "138" on front dj. Marginal lining on p. 139. Check marks on pp. 138, 140, 145.

"The answer is clearly that with his conversion Augustine did not 'become' a Christian, since he never had been a pagan" (marginal lining, p. 139).

"We see him gradually being led by encounter and inner development, by experience, thought, and act, until at last the hour of ultimate decision is there, by which the inner and the outer man, conscience and way of life, exhortation and active being meet in complete accord" (check mark, p. 140).

　　Bulletin, 5.27.61; *Reviews,* pp. 113–14.

147 AUGUSTINE. *The Mind and Heart of Augustine: A Biographical Sketch.* Compiled from Augustine's writings with explanatory notes by J. M. Flood. Introduction by M. C. D'Arcy, S.J. Fresno, Calif.: Academy Guild Press, 1960. 108 pp.

148 CATHERINE OF SIENA, SAINT. RAYMOND OF CAPUA, BLESSED. *The Life of St. Catherine of Siena.* Trans. George Lamb. New York: P. J. Kenedy and Sons, 1960; *S. Caterina da Siena* (Siena, 1934). 384 pp. Illus.

　　Bulletin, 3.18.61; *Reviews,* pp. 111–12.

149 JOHN OF THE CROSS, SAINT. BRUNO, FATHER, O.D.C. *St. John of the Cross.* Ed. Fr. Benedict Zimmerman, O.D.C. Introduction by Jacques Maritain. New York: Sheed and Ward, [1932]. 495 + xxxii pp.

　　O'Connor has marked "91" on back dj. Marginal lining, p. 91.

　　"Brother John also fought, but with love, not fire. The root of Martin Luther's error consists in an inordinate desire for sensible experiences of divine grace, a perversion of Tauler's mysticism—leading to a despair of ever being a *friend of God,* and to a search for salvation by a kind of faith—trust operating without good works and unvivified by charity. To this corruption of Christianity John of the Cross opposes the supernatural life in all its integrity—its supreme work of transformation and loving union with God. He begs us, by word and example, not to rest in the senses, which may deceive, but to abandon ourselves, wholly and entirely, to a pure, living faith, informed by charity and working by charity, a faith that is the sole proportionate means to a living union with God" (marginal lining, p. 91).

　　Bulletin, 12.21.57; *Reviews,* p. 46.

150 ———. Stein, Edith (Teresa Benedicta of the Cross, O.C.D.). *The Science of the Cross: A Study of St. John of the Cross.* Trans. Hilda Graef. Ed. Dr. L. Gelber and Fr. Romaeus Leuven, O.C.D. Preface by Dr. Lucy Gelber. Library of Living Catholic Thought. Chicago: Henry Regnery, 1960; *Kreuzeswissenschaft* (Louvain, n.d.). 243 + xxii pp.

Signed "F. O'Connor 1960." Brackets in text, p. 42.

"Hope empties the memory, since through it the latter is occupied with something not yet possessed" (bracketed, p. 42).

Bulletin, 10.1.60, p. 6; *Reviews,* pp. 96–97; *Letters,* p. 241.

151 Philip Neri, Saint. Bouyer, Louis de l'Oratoire. *The Roman Socrates: A Portrait of St. Philip Neri.* Trans. Michael Day, Cong. Orat. Westminster, Md.: Newman Press, 1958. 87 pp.

152 Thérèse of Lisieux. Saint. Robo, Etienne. *Two Portraits of St. Thérèse of Lisieux.* Chicago: Henry Regnery, 1955. 205 pp.

Signed, dated January 1956. Marginal linings, pp. 23, 28–29, 30, 31, 33, 34, 42, 156.

"Nature seemed to share my deep sadness; during those three days of despair there was not a ray of sunshine and the rain fell in torrents. Again and again I have noticed that all through my life nature has reflected my feelings" (marginal lining, p. 23).

"We should have, first of all, some idea of what is meant by faith if we are to understand what is meant by doubt. Faith, in a Catholic sense, is not just an opinion, a probability, a sentiment. It is an unshakable conviction that God has spoken to man, that His word is true and that it comes to us through the voice of the Church" (marginal lining, p. 156).

Bulletin, 5.26.56; *Reviews,* pp. 18–19; *Letters,* p. 135.

153 Vincent de Paul, Saint. Delarue, Jacques. *The Holiness of Vincent De Paul.* Trans. Suzanne Chapman. New York: P. J. Kenedy and Sons, 1960; *Sainteté de Monsieur Vincent* (n.p., 1959). 132 pp.

Bulletin, 7.11.63; *Reviews,* pp. 161–62.

154 ————. MATT, LEONARD VON, AND LOUIS COGNET. *St. Vincent de Paul*. Trans. Emma Craufurd. Chicago: Henry Regnery, 1960. [240] pp. Photographs. W/o dj.
  Bulletin, 7.11.63; *Reviews*, pp. 161–62.

155 MARITAIN, JACQUES. *The Sin of the Angel: An Essay on a Re-Interpretation of Some Thomistic Positions*. Trans. William L. Rossner, S.J. Westminster, Md.: Newman Press, 1959; "Le péché l'Ange," *de Revue Thomiste* (1956), no. 2. 106 + xv pp.

156 ROUGEMONT, DENIS DE. *The Devil's Share: An Essay on the Diabolic in Modern Society*. Trans. Haakon Chevalier. New York: Meridian M21, 1956 (New York, 1944). 221 + viii pp. Pap.
  Signed, dated 1960. Marginal linings, pp. 75, 98.

157 GLEASON, ROBERT W., S.J. *The World to Come*. New York: Sheed and Ward, 1958. 172 pp.
  Signed, dated 1959. Marginal lining on p. 162. Marginalia: "Tielhard de Chardin," p. 164.
  "The Church is Christ Himself progressively assuming all humanity into union with Himself, and the material universe is touched by this activity and redeemed by it. Christ, who directs the evolutionary process, is the soul of the movement bearing human history towards its term, and He sculpts in time the face of God upon humanity. There is, as St. Augustine has pointed out, 'one great man, the total Christ, growing through the centuries to His full stature.' In this redemption, we must recall constantly that the corporal, the biological, the cosmological has its place. Biology discovers to us constantly the intimate bonds which tie man to his universe" (passage marked "Tielhard de Chardin," p. 164).
  Bulletin, 8.22.59; *Reviews*, pp. 75–76.

158 RAHNER, KARL. *On the Theology of Death*. Trans., with a preface, by Charles H. Henkey, S.T.D. Quaestiones Disputatae. New York: Herder and Herder, 1963; *Zur Theologie des Todes* (Freiburg, 1961). 127 pp. Pap.
  Signed on inside cover, dated 1963.

Letters, pp. 520–21, 527.

159 CATHERINE OF GENOA, SAINT. *Treatise on Purgatory: The Dialogue*. Trans. Charlotte Balfour and Helen Douglas Irvine. London: Sheed and Ward, 1946. 142 + xv pp. W/o dj.

Signed, dated 1949.

Letters, pp. 113, 118, 121.

160 LACKMANN, MAX. *The Augsburg Confession and Catholic Unity*. Trans. Walter R. Bouman. Preface by Gustave Weigel. New York: Herder and Herder, 1963; *Katholische Einheit und Ausburger Konfession* (Graz, 1959). 159 + xv pp.

Signed, dated 1963. O'Connor's numbers on dj: "14 18 24 26 29 32 40 74 77* 78 85 103 107* 120 138." Marginal linings on pp. 9, 14, 18, 19, 23, 24, 26, 29, 39, 40, 74, 77, 78, 85, 103, 105, 107, 119, 122, 129, 138–39. Check marks on pp. 25, 32, 107. Marginal marking, p. 59. Correction of text, p. 97.

Letters, p. 525.

161 KNOX, RONALD A. *In Soft Garments: A Collection of Oxford Conferences*. New York: Sheed and Ward, 1953 (1942). 214 + ix pp.

O'Connor's number on dj: "183." Marginal linings on pp. 86, 87, 91, 107. Check marks on pp. 89, 183.

"The Protestant only feels his religion to be true as long as he goes on practising it; the Catholic feels the truth of his religion as something independent of himself, which does not cease to be valid when he, personally, fails to live up to its precepts" (marginal lining, p. 87).

". . . the Catholic who lives carelessly commits, in however slight a degree, an added sin of scandal" (checked, p. 89).

Bulletin, 8.4.56; *Reviews*, pp. 24–25.

162 MAURIAC, FRANÇOIS. *What I Believe*. Trans., with an introduction, by Wallace Fowlie. New York: Farrar, Straus and Cudahy, 1963; *Ce Que Je Crois* (Paris, 1962). 139 + xviii pp.

Signed, dated 1963.

Letters, p. 589.

163 BOUYER OF THE ORATORY, LOUIS. *Christian Initiation.* Trans. J. R. Foster. New York: Macmillan, 1960; *L'Initiation chrétienne* (Paris, n.d.). 148 pp.

> *Bulletin,* 11.12.60; *Reviews,* p. 101.

164 GLEASON, ROBERT W., S.J. ED. *The Study of Scripture.* New York: Paulist Press, 1962 (New York, 1962). 24 pp. Pap. Pamphlet.

> From *In the Eyes of Others,* ed. Gleason.

165 JONE, REV. HERIBERT, O.F.M. CAP., J.C.D. *Moral Theology.* Trans. Rev. Urban Adelman, O.F.M. Cap., J.C.D. Westminster, Md.: Newman Press, 1961; *Moral Theologie* (Paderborn, 1929). 610 + xxi pp.

> Sacraments, canon law, and practices of the Roman Catholic Church. "This edition of *Moral Theology* is revised in accordance with the sixteenth German edition and contains additions that will appear in the seventeenth." The book "AIMS TO PROVIDE . . . THE EDUCATED LAITY with a clear explanation of the teachings of the Catholic Church on moral matters, and thus enable them to help themselves in solving many of the minor problems of conscience that occur in their daily lives" (front dj).

166 SMEDT, EMILE-JOSEPH DE. *The Priesthood of the Faithful.* Trans. Joseph M. F. Marique, S.J. New York: Paulist Press, Deus Books, 1962. 126 pp. Pap.

> "Pastoral Letter Addressed to Priests, Religious and Lay Apostles of the Diocese of Bruges" by the Bishop of Bruges.

167 BERGSON, HENRI. *The Two Sources of Morality and Religion.* Trans. R. Ashley Audra and Cloudesley Brereton, with the assistance of W. Horsfall Carter. Garden City, N.Y.: Doubleday, Anchor A28, 1954. 320 pp. Pap.

168 KNOX, RONALD. *Lightning Meditations.* New York: Sheed and Ward, 1959. 164 + x pp.

> Flyleaf signed "To Flannery with a blessing from *Father Paul.*"

169 CATHERINE OF SIENA, SAINT. *The Dialogue of the Seraphic Vir-*

gin Catherine of Siena. Trans., with an introduction of Saint Catherine's life and times, by Algar Thorold. New and abridged ed. Westminster, Md.: Newman Bookshop, 1944. 344 pp.

"Dictated by her, while in a state of ecstasy, to her secretaries, and completed in the year of our lord 1370" with an eye-witness account of her death.

Signed, dated 1949.

Letters, p. 133.

170 FRANCIS DE SALES, SAINT. *Introduction to a Devout Life.* Revised and corrected by Rev. J. M. Lelen. Foreword by Rev. E. J. Carney, O.S.F.S., S.T.D. New York: Catholic Book Publishing, [1946]. 447 pp.

Abstract of the life of Saint Francis is prefixed.

171 MOUROUX, JEAN. *The Christian Experience: An Introduction to a Theology.* Trans. George Lamb. New York: Sheed and Ward, 1954. 370 + xi pp.

172 GUARDINI, ROMANO. *The Rosary of Our Lady.* Trans. H. von Schuecking. New York: P. J. Kenedy and Sons, [1955]. 94 pp.

O'Connor's numbers on back dj: "31 35 47 52." Marginal linings on pp. 31, 52. Underlinings on pp. 17, 20, 35. Check mark on p. 47.

Bulletin, 4.28.56; *Reviews,* pp. 16–17; *Letters,* p. 150.

173 CHRISTIAN. *Christian Asceticism and Modern Man.* Trans. Walter Mitchell and the Carisbrooke Dominicans. New York: Philosophical Library, 1955; *L'Ascèse Chrétienne et l'Homme Contemporain* (n.p., n.d.). 262 + xi pp.

Signed, dated January 1959. O'Connor's numbers on front dj: "191 204 259." Marginal linings on pp. 191, 204–5, 258, 259, 262.

Review unpublished.

174 FÉNELON (ARCHBISHOP FRANÇOIS DE SALIGNAC DE LA MOTHE). *Fénelon's Letters to Men and Women.* Selected, with an introduction, by Derek Stanford. Westminster, Md.: Newman Press, 1957. 208 pp.

O'Connor notes on back dj: "73 28on style 102." Marginal linings on pp. 83, 84, 103.

"He often speaks to those who listen faithfully; and when we do not hear His secret, familiar Voice within, it is a proof that we do not hush ourselves duly to hearken" (marginal lining, p. 84).

Bulletin, 10.26.57; *Reviews,* pp. 44–45.

175 POURRAT, REV. PIERRE. *Christian Spirituality.* Vol. 1, *From the Time of our Lord till the Dawn of the Middle Ages,* trans. W. H. Mitchell and S. P. Jacques. Westminster, Md.: Newman Press, 1953 (1927). 312 + x pp. W/o dj.

Author is Supérieur du Grand Séminaire de Lyon.

176 ———. *Christian Spirituality.* Vol. 2, *In the Middle Ages,* trans. S. P. Jacques. Westminster, Md.: Newman Press, 1953 (1927). 341 + xiii pp.

Marginalia: "Bonaventura," p. 181.

177 ———. *Christian Spirituality.* Vol. 3, *Later Developments; Part 1, From the Renaissance to Jansenism,* trans. W. H. Mitchell. Westminster, Md.: Newman Press, 1953 (1927). 405 + xii pp.

178 ———. *Christian Spirituality.* Vol. 4, *Later Developments; Part 2, From Jansenism to Modern Times,* trans. Donald Attwater. Westminster, Md.: Newman Press, 1955. 549 + [xvii] pp.

179 WEIL, SIMONE. *Waiting for God.* Trans. Emma Craufurd. Introduction by Leslie A. Fiedler. New York: G. P. Putnam's Sons, [1951]. 227 + xi pp.

Letters, pp. 105, 106, 109, 522.

180 COLLEDGE, ERIC, ED. *The Mediaeval Mystics of England.* New York: Charles Scribner's Sons, [1961]. 309 pp.

An anthology of selections of writings by medieval mystics. Introduction by Colledge. General editor, Elmer O'Brien, S.J.

Bulletin, 9.30.61; *Reviews,* p. 122.

181 DE LA BEDOYÈRE, MICHAEL. *The Archbishop and the Lady: The Story of Fénelon and Madame Guyon.* New York: Pantheon, [1956]. 256 pp.

O'Connor's numbers of dj: "84 136 150–1 185 227 224."
Marginal linings on pp. 84, 98, 150, 151, 185, 227, 250.

Review unpublished; *Letters,* pp. 165–66, 167, 207.

182 MEISTER ECKHART. BLAKNEY, RAYMOND BERNARD. *Meister Eckhart: A Modern Translation.* New York: Harper and Brothers, Harper Torchbooks TB 8, 1957 [New York, 1941]. 333 + xxviii pp. Pap.

Letters, p. 297.

183 THURSTON, HERBERT, S.J. *The Physical Phenomena of Mysticism.* Ed. J. H. Crehan, S.J. London: Burns Oates, 1952. 419 pp.

184 UNDERHILL, EVELYN. *Mysticism: A Study in the Nature and Development of Man's Spiritual Consciousness.* New York: Noonday Press, Meridian MG 1, 1955. 519 + xviii pp. Pap.

Letters, pp. 116, 297.

185 GRAEF, HILDA. *Mystics of Our Times.* Garden City, N.Y.: Doubleday, Hanover House, 1962. 240 pp. W/o dj.

Chapter 10 is on Pierre Teilhard de Chardin.

Bulletin, 8.18.62; *Reviews,* pp. 148–49.

186 BOUYER, REV. LOUIS. *The Spirit and Forms of Protestantism.* Trans. A. V. Littledale. Westminster, Md.: Newman Press, 1956. 234 + xiii pp.

Signed, dated 1957. Marginal linings on pp. 82, 88, 93, 94, 152, 153, 157, 158, 161, 164, 193, 194. Underlinings on pp. 157, 158, 196.

"The disposition required for union with God does not consist in understanding, tasting, feeling, or imagining God; it consists solely of purity and love, that is, of *complete submission of the will and absolute detachment from all for the sake of God alone*" (quoting Saint John of the Cross; marginal lining, p. 94).

Bulletin, 4.27.57; *Reviews,* pp. 35–36.

187 MERTON, THOMAS. *Thoughts in Solitude.* New York: Farrar, Straus and Cudahy, 1958. 124 pp.

188 GOLDBRUNNER, JOSEF. *Holiness Is Wholeness.* Trans. Stanley

Goodman. New York: Pantheon, [1955]; *Heiligkeit und Ge-sundheit* (Freiburg, n.d.). 63 pp.

Signed, dated 1955. Marginal lining on p. 33.

189 KNOX, RONALD. WAUGH, EVELYN. *Monsignor Ronald Knox.* Boston: Little, Brown, [1959]. [358] pp.

Compiled by Waugh from original sources.

190 MERTON, THOMAS. *The Sign of Jonas.* New York: Harcourt, Brace, [1953]. 362 pp.

191 TEILHARD DE CHARDIN, PIERRE. CORTE, NICHOLAS. *Pierre Teilhard de Chardin: His Life and Spirit* [*La vie et l'âme de Teilhard de Chardin*]. Trans. Martin Jarrett-Kerr, C.R. New York: Macmillan, 1960 (1957). 120 + xx pp.

Signed, dated 1960. Marginal linings on pp. 8, 97, 100. Marginal marking on p. 96.

Bulletin, 10.15.60, p. 3; *Reviews*, p. 99.

192 ———. Copy 2. Second printing, 1961.

193 ———. *Letters from a Traveller* (*Lettres de Voyage, 1923–39* and *Nouvelles Lettres de Voyage, 1939–55*). Trans. René Hague, Violet Hammersley, Barbara Wall, and Nöel Lindsay. General editor, Bernard Wall. Introduction by Sir Julian Huxley, F.R.S.; Pierre Leroy, S.J.; and Claude Aragonnès. New York: Harper and Brothers, [1962] (1956). 380 pp. Illus. Map. W/o dj.

Signed, 1962.

Southern Cross, 4.27.63; *Reviews*, pp. 160–61.

194 ———. RABUT, OLIVIER, O.P. *Teilhard De Chardin: A Critical Study.* New York: Sheed and Ward, [1961]; *Dialogue avec Teilhard de Chardin* (Paris, n.d.). 247 pp.

Signed, dated 1961. Check marks on pp. 38, 66, 69, 130, 146, 152, 160, 166, 187, 207, 208, 242.

"There is a danger in wanting to make the mysteries of Christianity more tangible, for their reality is not of a kind that can be handled. Physical realities have spiritual bearings; but the central reality of religion is not of the same stuff as even human evolution" (marginal notation, p. 208).

Bulletin, 12.23.61; *Reviews*, pp. 126–27.

195 ———. RAVEN, CHARLES E. *Teilhard de Chardin: Scientist and Seer*. New York: Harper and Row, [1962]. 221 pp.

Signed, dated 1963. Marginal markings on pp. 39, 47, 82, 85, 87, 88, 92, 97, 136, 155, 185. Check marks on pp. 51, 65, 76, 91, 186.

"Where Bergson recognised an initial instinct and a progressively estranged intellect, Teilhard saw a primal energy developing into fuller and more expressive perceptions and a more coherent and effective activity" (marginal lining, p. 39).

". . . it was in the pursuit of his secular activities and the service and friendship of his neighbours that he realised the presence of Christ as not only the embodiment of the divine-human unity, but the source and goal of evolution, the inspiration of man's adventure and the instrument of his individual and social integration" (pp. 76–77; check mark on p. 76).

"Democracy, the eldest child of the French Revolution, has a boundless faith in the future, but it has mistaken equality for liberty and the crowd for the community" (marginal lining, p. 87).

"Roman Catholicism was saved from this reaction by the strength and vitality of its Thomist inheritance. Though Existentialism owed its origin to the disillusionment and pessimism of the time, and it its quality had some affinity with Protestant neo-orthodoxy, it did not infect the wisdom or challenge the tradition established by the great Schoolmen of the thirteenth century, and in the last thirty years restated by a number of scholars. The best known of them, Étienne Gilson and Jacques Maritain, held the field all over the world and indeed initiated important attempts to apply the principles of St. Thomas to the modern problems raised by science and sociology. Though the doctrinal innovation and official policy of the Vatican made it evident that no concession to liberalism could be expected, at least an enlightened Scholasticism saved most churchmen from the sort of frustration which the contrast between the immensity of our opportunity and the inadequacy of our equipment made almost inevitable. If under the circumstances Rome could not at once endorse or authorise Teilhard's message, at least it did not condemn him—except to silence. It waited on the event, without (it appears) any recognition of its importance!" (marginal lining, p. 155).

"Like St. Paul, Teilhard saw all things as 'in Christ'—and that not figuratively but factually" (check marks, both sides of p. 186).

196 TROELTSCH, ERNST. *Christian Thought: Its History and Application.* Edited, with an introduction, by Baron F. von Hügel. New York: Meridian, Living Age LA 12, 1957. 191 pp. Pap.

Marginal linings on pp. 27, 28.

"Baptism is the all-important fact of our attainment to personality, in the first instance all but entirely, and up to the end very largely, through our birth and incorporation into a world of realized values, a world already awake to and penetrated by that spiritual life which, as yet, only slumbers within ourselves. I greatly wish that the later over-absorption in the individual contribution (real though it certainly is in conviction of every kind) had not pushed so very much aside this great insight" (marginal lining, von Hügel's introduction, p. 27).

"What, from the first, gained more men to faith than probably all other reasons put together is surely the evidence, standing clear before them, of the practical, indeed also the speculative, fruitfulness of such faith in the believers known to them" (marginal lining, von Hügel's introduction, p. 28).

197 COWAN, WAYNE H., ED. *What the Christian Hopes For in Society.* Foreword by Reinhold Niebuhr. Reflection Book. New York: Association Press, [1957]. 125 pp. Pap.

Selections from *Christianity and Crisis.*

198 D'ARCY, M. C. *Communism and Christianity.* Harmondsworth, England: Penguin S163, 1956. [191] pp. Pap.

199 TAWNEY, R. H. *Religion and the Rise of Capitalism: A Historical
Study.* New York: New American Library, Mentor M22,
1952 (New York, 1926). 280 pp. Pap.

Holland Memorial Lectures, 1922.

200 WEIGEL, GUSTAVE, S.J. *Catholic Theology in Dialogue.* New
York: Harper and Brothers, 1961. 126 pp.

On flyleaf: "May—1964. For Flannery, 'Only in penetrat-
ing into this great Shekinah, past and present, shall we see
the back of God.'—G. Weigel—66 Light-Joy Janet."

201 LEO XIII. KEIFER, BROTHER WILLIAM J., S.M. MARIANIST.
Leo XIII: A Light from Heaven. Milwaukee: Bruce Publishing,
[1961]. 222 + xii pp. Illus.

Southern Cross, 10.31.63; *Reviews,* pp. 165–66.

202 HÜGEL, FRIEDRICH VON. *Some Notes on the Petrine Claims.*
London: Sheed and Ward, 1930. 103 + viii pp.

Signed.

Letters, p. 236.

203 NEWMAN, JOHN HENRY CARDINAL. *Apologia pro Vita Sua.*
Introduction by Anton C. Pegis. New York: Modern Library
113, 1950. 430 + xiv pp.

Marginal linings on pp. 121 (reference to Augustine), 122,
203.

"Whether the ideas of the coming age upon religion were
true or false, they would be real. 'In the present day,' I said,
'mistiness is the mother of wisdom. A man who can set
down half-a-dozen general propositions, which escape from
destroying one another only by being diluted into truisms,
who can hold the balance between opposites so skilfully as to
do without fulcrum or beam, who never enunciates a truth
without guarding himself against being supposed to exclude
the contradictory,—who holds that Scripture is the only authority, yet that the Church is to be deferred to, that faith
only justifies, yet that it does not justify without works, that

grace does not depend on the sacraments, yet is not given without them, that bishops are a divine ordinance, yet those who have them not are in the same religious condition as those who have,—this is your safe man and the hope of the Church; this is what the Church is said to want, not party men, but sensible, temperate, sober, well-judging persons, to guide it through the channel of no-meaning, between the Scylla and Charybdis of Aye and No" (marginal lining, p. 122).

"Only this I know full well now, and did not know then, that the Catholic Church allows no image of any sort, material or immaterial, no dogmatic symbol, no rite, no sacrament, no Saint, not even the Blessed Virgin herself, to come between the soul and its Creator. It is face to face, 'solus cum solo,' in all matters between man and his God. He alone creates; He also has redeemed; before His awful eyes we go in death; in the vision of Him is our eternal beatitude" (marginal lining, p. 203).

204 ———. Bouyer, Louis. *Newman: His Life and Spirituality.* Trans. J. Lewis May. New York: Meridian M87, 1960; *Newman: Sa Vie: Sa Spiritualité* (London, 1958; Paris, n.d.). 391 + xiii pp. Pap.

Marginal lining on p. 293. Pages 107–12 held by paper clip.

205 ———. *Letters of John Henry Newman.* Selected and ed., with an introduction, by Derek Stanford and Muriel Spark. Westminster, Md.: Newman Press, 1957. 251 pp.

Marginal notation on p. 105.

206 ———. O'Faoláin, Seán. *Newman's Way: The Odyssey of John Henry Newman.* New York: Devin-Adair, 1952. 335 + [xv] pp. Illus.

Letters, p. 55.

207 Rosmini. Leetham, Claude. *Rosmini: Priest, Philosopher and Patriot.* Introduction by Giuseppe Bozzetti. Baltimore: Helicon Press, 1958 (1957). 508 + xxiii pp. Map.

O'Connor's note on front dj: "108 127 137Jansenism 142

152 266 272 319." Marginal linings on pp. 116, 127, 142, 152, 270, 272, 319. Marginal notations on pp. 116, 266. Correction of text, p. 138.

"No principle, good or bad, remains for long in the human mind without in the course of time producing the consequences that are its logical result" (marginal check, p. 116).

"We must remember that our state of contemplation must not be a state of inertia, but a state of preparation, a state in which we accumulate fervour, generosity, grace, so as to be ready and eager for any work to which the Lord may call us. We should be in our retirement like lions in their den; we should meditate in our house like taut bows, like wine in a bottle, like a force under pressure, so that in due time we may expand and burst forth.

"Try to implant in all the brethren an unlimited love of truth and of all good. If there is in us a great prevailing love of truth, we shall find it everywhere, we shall always be happy when we find it. So if we have a perfect love of good we shall love it wherever we find it, in every person, in every circumstance, under every shape. The law of love is beautiful: it hates none, it has no envy, it seeks only good" (marginal lining, p. 142).

Bulletin, 11.14.59; *Reviews*, pp. 78–79.

208 SPELLMAN, CARDINAL FRANCIS. GANNON, ROBERT I., S.J. *The Cardinal Spellman Story*. Garden City, N.Y.: Doubleday, 1962. 447 + vi pp. Illus.

Bulletin, 8.4.62; *Reviews*, pp. 147–48.

209 STRITCH, CARDINAL SAMUEL. BUEHRLE, MARIE CECILIA. *The Cardinal Stritch Story*. [Milwaukee]: Bruce Publishing, 1960 (1959). 197 + xii pp. Illus.

Southern Cross, 10.31.63; *Reviews*, p. 165.

210 GUARDINI, ROMANO. *Meditations before Mass*. Trans. Elinor Castendyk Briefs. Westminster, Md.: Newman Press, 1956 (1955); *Besinnung vor der Feier der Heiligen Messe* (Mainz, n.d.). 203 + xiv pp.

O'Connor's notes on back dj: "22 42 73 91 aim96 104f 160 180." Marginal linings on pp. 22, 47, 73, 91, 96, 104–5, 106, 180. Underlining on p. 160. Check mark on p. 161.

"There is a beautiful expression for this in Italian: *'faro atto di presenza,'* to perform the act of *being present*" (marginal lining, p. 22).

"So it is in the Church. The altar is not an allegory, but a symbol. The thoughtful believer does not have to be taught that it is a border, that 'above it' stretch inaccessible heights and 'beyond it' the reaches of divine remoteness; somehow he is aware of this.

"To grasp the mystery all that is necessary on the part of the believer is intrinsic readiness and calm reflection; then his heart will respond with reverence. In a very vital hour he may even have an experience somewhat similar to that of Moses when he guarded his flocks in the loneliness of Mount Horeb. Suddenly 'The Lord appeared to him in a flame of fire out of the midst of a bush: and he saw that the bush was on fire and was not burnt. And Moses said: I will go and see this great sight, why the bush is not burnt. And when the Lord saw that he went forward to see, he called to him out of the midst of the bush, and said: Moses, Moses. And he answered: Here I am. And he said: Come not nigh hither. Put off the shoes from thy feet; for the place whereon thou standest is holy ground' (Exodus 3:2–5)" (p. 42, unmarked page noted on dj).

"The true congregation is a gathering of those who belong to Christ, the holy people of God, united by faith and love. Essentially, it is of His making, a piece of new creation, which finds expression in the bearing of its participants" (marginal lining, p. 91).

"The early Christians believed that it was proper to clothe the sacred in mystery. One reason for their attitude was the danger of persecution, which profaned it at every opportunity; but they also knew that mystery is the natural element of holiness" (marginal lining and check mark, p. 106).

"When a man accepts divine truth in the obedience of faith, he is forced to re-think human truth" (underlining and marginal lining, p. 160).

"Not that it shuns it or shies away from it, but it is remarkable how readily piety slides off into fantasy, sentimentality and exaggeration. Legends and devotional books offer only too frequent and devastating proof of this; unfortunately piety is inclined to lose itself in the subjective, to become musty, turgid, *unspiritual*. Divine reality is never any of these, never falsely spiritual in the sense of the vaporous, the unsubstantial. Divine reality, which is another name for truth, remains as divinely substantial as the living Jesus who walked the earth. But it must be illuminated by the spirit, the Holy Spirit" (marginal lining, p. 180).

Bulletin, 11.24.56; *Reviews*, p. 28.

211 ———. *Prayer in Practice*. Trans. Prince Leopold of Loewenstein-Wertheim. New York: Pantheon, [1957]; *Vorschule des Betens* (Mainz, n.d.). 228 + vi pp.

O'Connor's numbers on dj: "126 148 162 167–8." Marginal linings on pp. 126–27, 148, 162, 163, 167, 168.

Bulletin, 2.22.56; *Reviews*, pp. 52–53.

212 JOHNSON, SAMUEL. *Doctor Johnson's Prayers*. Ed. Elton Trueblood. New York: Harper and Brothers, [1947]. 66 + xxxv pp.

Hand set in Weiss type by Arthur Rushmore and Edna Rushmore at the Golden Hind Press in Madison, New Jersey.

213 CREHAN, JOSEPH, S.J. *Early Christian Baptism and the Creed: A Study in Ante-Nicene Theology*. Bellarmine Series, no. 13. London: Burns Oates and Washbourne, 1950. 189 + x pp. Pap.

214 GUARDINI, ROMANO. *Prayers from Theology*. Trans. Richard Newnham. New York: Herder and Herder, 1959; *Theologische Gebete* (Frankfurt am Main, n.d.). [62] pp.

Includes prayers on "The Mystery of Grace," pp. 19–21; "Recognizing Christ," pp. 32–33; "Understanding the Redemption," pp. 36–42; and "The Judgment," pp. 59–60.

215 ———. *Sacred Signs (Von Heiligen Zeichen)*. Trans. Grace Branham. St. Louis, Mo.: Pio Decimo Press, [1956]. 106 pp. Pap. Illus.

   Includes essays on "Fire," pp. 49–51; "Light and Heat," pp. 61–64, and "Time Sanctified," pp. 93–99.

216 BOSSUET, JAMES BENIGN, BISHOP OF MEAUX. *History of the Variations of the Protestant Churches.* Vol. 1. Trans. from French. New York: D. and J. Sadlier, [1845]. 372 pp. W/o dj.

   Flyleaf signed "D. A. Cook, 1872." Half-title page signed "Hugh Cline from Mrs. Cook—." Sticker on flyleaf reads, "Mrs. H. J. Cook, Albany, Dougherty Co." Loose binding.

217 HUGHES, PHILIP. *A Popular History of the Reformation.* Garden City, N.Y.: Hanover House, [1957]. 343 pp.

   Bulletin, 6.8.57; *Reviews,* pp. 37–38.

218 KNOX, R.A. *Enthusiasm: A Chapter in the History of Religion.* Special reference to the seventeenth and eighteenth centuries. Preface by Evelyn Waugh. Oxford: Clarendon Press, 1959 (1950). 622 + viii pp.

   Signed, dated 1961.

219 HUGHES, PHILIP. *The Reformation in England.* Vol. 1, *The King's Proceedings.* New York: Macmillan, 1951. 404 + xxi pp. Illus. Maps.

   O'Connor's note on back dj: "20 26 185."

   Letters, p. 31.

220 RYNNE, XAVIER. *Letters from Vatican City: Vatican Council II (First Session): Background and Debates.* New York: Farrar, Straus and Cudahy, [1963]. 289 + xiii pp. Illus.

   Letters, p. 583.

221 TAVARD, GEORGE. *Protestant Hopes and the Catholic Responsibility.* Notre Dame, Ind.: Fides Publishers, [1960]. 63 pp. Pap. Pamphlet.

   "Discussion club text" based on two lectures given by Father Tavard for Adult Education Centers, the Archdiocese of Chicago, in 1959.

222 FREMANTLE, ANNE, ED. *A Treasury of Early Christianity.* In-

troduction by Fremantle. New York: Viking Press, 1953. 625 + xiv pp.

Anthology of writings.

223 ENGLAND, THE RIGHT REV. JOHN. *The Works of the Right Rev. John England, First Bishop of Charleston.* Vol. 1, ed. the Right Rev. Ignatius Aloysius Reynolds. Baltimore: John Murphy, 1849. 505 + vii pp. W/o dj.

Heavily foxed. Torn spine.

Signed "John Treanor" on first blank page.

224 ———. *The Works of the Right Rev. John England, First Bishop of Charleston.* Vol. 5, ed. the Right Rev. Ignatius Aloysius Reynolds. Baltimore: John Murphy, 1849. [517] + xii pp.

Heavily foxed.

Marking: "Why dont the" in O'Connor's hand on first blank page.

225 THOMAS AQUINAS, SAINT. *Introduction to Saint Thomas Aquinas.* Ed., with an introduction, by Anton C. Pagis. New York: Modern Library 259, [1948]. 690 + xxx pp.

Signed, dated 1953. Marginal linings on pp. xxiv, xxvi, xxvii, 18, 92, 142, 143. Underlinings on pp. xxiii, 17, 80, 86, 93, 142.

"Man as a knower must be partly material in order to be adequately a knower. Of course, such a notion is bound to sound scandalous to modern ears. For we are the heirs of generations of philosophic speculations according to which man is a *thinker* and a *mind.* Now it is a fact that the Thomistic man is a knower rather than a thinker, and he is a composite being rather than a mind. In fact, St. Thomas does not even have in his vocabulary a term corresponding to the term thinker: you cannot translate such a term into Thomistic Latin. If we are to judge matters as St. Thomas has done, we are bound to say that the European man became a thinker after he ruined himself as a knower; and we can now even trace the steps of that ruination—from Augustinian Platonism to the nominalistic isolationism of Ockham to the despairing and desperate methodism of Descartes. For what we call the decline of mediaeval philosophy was really a transition from man as a knower to man as a thinker—from man knowing the world of sensible things to man thinking abstract thoughts in separation from existence. What is thinking but dis-existentialized knowing?" (underlining p. xxiii and marginal lining, p. xxiv, in Pegis's introduction).

"Man as a knower must be such that he can give existence, within his knowledge, not to abstract essences, but to sensible beings. That is why man as a knower needs a body; for, through the senses of his body he can give sensible existence in the order of knowing to that which is sensible in the order of being. The body as part of the knowing man answers for St. Thomas Aquinas the two questions which knowledge poses for him. In knowing sensible being, how do we know it as sensible, which it is, and as being, which it likewise is?" (marginal lining, p. xxvi, in Pegis's introduction).

"In other words, being (the being of and in sensible things) first comes to us in the way that it is, as sensible actuality, and human knowing begins by being the exercise by man of the sensible act of being in things" (marginal lining, p. xxvii, in Pegis's introduction).

". . . and its truth so far remains that it does not allow the minds of those to whom the revelation has been made, to rest in the likenesses, but raises them to the knowledge of intelligible truths" (underlining, p. 17).

"The very hiding of truth in figures is useful for the exercise of thoughtful minds, and as a defense against the ridicule of the unbelievers, according to the words, *Give not that which is holy to dogs (Matt.* vii [7:6])" (underlining, p. 17).

"*On the contrary,* Gregory says: *Holy Scripture by the manner of its speech transcends every science, because in one and the same sentence, while it describes a fact, it reveals a mystery*" (marginal lining, p. 18).

Letters, pp. 93–94, 97, 103, 104, 107, 258, 306, 308, 335, 365, 367.

226 AUGUSTINE, SAINT. *The Confessions of Saint Augustine.* Trans. Edward B. Pusey. Introduction by Harold C. Gardiner, S.J. Cardinal Edition C-27. New York: Pocket Books, 1952. 301 + xiv pp. Pap.

Sticker on title page: "Miss Viola Berry, 419 Sinclair Avenue, N.E., Atlanta, Georgia." Marginal linings on pp. 3, 35, 68, 90 (double). Underlinings on pp. 10, 68, 92. Correction of text, p. 21.

"Yet woe to him that speaketh not, since mute are even the most eloquent" (marginal lining, p. 3).

". . . deliver those too who call not on Thee yet, that they may call on Thee, and Thou mayest deliver them" (underlining, p. 10).

"But behold, I see a thing not understood by the proud, nor laid open to children, lowly in access, in its recesses lofty, and veiled with mysteries; and I was not such as could enter into it, or stoop my neck to follow its steps. For not as I know speak, did I feel when I turned to those Scriptures; but they seemed to me unworthy to be compared to the stateliness of Tully: for my swelling pride shrunk from their lowliness, nor could my sharp wit pierce the interior thereof. Yet were they such as would grow up in a little one. But I disdained to be a little one; and, swollen with pride, took myself to be a great one" (marginal lining, p. 35).

". . . so a believer, whose all this world of wealth is, and who having nothing, yet possesseth all things, by cleaving unto Thee, whom all things serve, though he know not even the circles of the Great Bear, yet is it folly to doubt but he is in a better state than one who can measure the heavens, and number the stars, and poise the elements, yet neglecteth Thee who has made all things in number, weight, and measure" (marginal lining, p. 68).

". . . while it [Scripture] lay open to all to read, it reserved the majesty of its mysteries within its profounder
meaning, stooping to all in the great plainness of its words
and lowliness of its style, yet calling forth the intensest
application of such as are not light of heart; that so it might
receive all in its open bosom" (double marginal lining,
p. 90).

"towardliness to virtue" (underlining, p. 92).

Letters, p. 128.

227 HIERONYMUS, SAINT. *The Satirical Letters of St. Jerome.* Trans.
Paul Carroll. Gateway Edition 6020. Chicago: Henry Regnery, n.d. 198 pp. Pap.

"Miscellaneous Letters" added. Misbound. Title page
missing.

O'Connor's note facing p. 1: " 'I like the rule that corrects
the emotion.' Braque." Marginal lining, p. 3.

228 PAYNE, ROBERT. *The Holy Fire: The Story of the Fathers of the
Eastern Church.* New York: Harper and Brothers, 1957. 313
+ xxii pp. Illus. Maps.

Marginal lining on pp. xiii, xx (double). Marginal notation
on pp. xii, xiv, xvi, xvii.

Bulletin, 7.20.57; *Reviews,* p. 40.

229 SIMON, REV. PAUL. *The Human Element in the Church of
Christ.* Trans. Meyrick Booth. Westminster, Md.: Newman
Press, 1954; *Das Menschliche in der Kirche* (Freiburg, n.d.).
166 + ix pp.

230 LAWLER, JUSTUS GEORGE. *The Christian Imagination: Studies in
Religious Thought.* Introduction by Rev. John M. Oesterreicher. Westminster, Md.: Newman Press, 1955. 199 + xxiv pp.

Marginal linings on pp. 38, 56. Marginalia: "Conrad:
'Highest possible justice to the visible universe,' " p. 38.

"It was a serious error in those of whom Augustine
speaks to assume that it does not matter what men think of
the created universe so long as they think rightly concerning God. For error in the matter of the universe means false

opinion about God" (quoting Aquinas; marginal lining, p. 38, with annotated quotation from Fr. Conrad Pepler).

"Perhaps this rather delicate subject of sacramentalized nature, because it rests on so subtle a foundation, can be clarified by the following parallel: just as in man there must be intelligence before there can be faith, just as the gifts of the Holy Spirit must be present in a vague, passive manner in the soul before there can be true contemplation, so it is fitting that there be in matter, before it can be ennobled in the last day, a certain unactualized splendor which renders possible this future reception of excellence. Man, recognizing this disposition toward the perfection of its nature, treats matter with a view to its worth, in a manner analogous to that whereby Christians treat infidels with reverence because they are potentially members of the Mystical Body. Now it is this 'potency' in matter that is one reason for speaking of the sacramental aspect of nature" (marginal lining, p. 56).

231 VON HILDEBRAND, DIETRICH. *The New Tower of Babel.* New York: P. J. Kenedy and Sons, [1953]. 243 pp.

232 WHITE, VICTOR, O.P., S.T.M. *God the Unknown and Other Essays.* New York: Harper and Brothers, 1956. 205 + viii pp.

Signed, dated March 1957.

Bulletin, 6.8.57; *Reviews,* pp. 38–39.

233 HUGHES, PHILIP. *A Popular History of the Catholic Church.* Garden City, N.Y.: Doubleday, Image D4, 1955. (New York, 1949). 309 + ix pp. Pap. Tables.

Stamped "NOTRE DAME BOOK SHOP, SAVANNAH, GEORGIA."

234 RICE, EDWARD. *The Church: A Pictorial History.* New York: Farrar, Straus and Cudahy, 1961. 268 pp. Illus.

235 CHRIST, FRANK L., AND GERARD E. SHERRY, EDS. *American Catholicism and the Intellectual Ideal.* Preface by John Wright, bishop of Pittsburgh. New York: Appleton-Century-Crofts, [1961]. 318 + xxv pp. Pap.

Anthology.

Flyleaf reads, "To Miss O'Connor with kindest personal regards Gerry Sherry."

236 RAHILL, PETER J. *The Catholic in America: From Colonial Times to the Present Day.* Chicago: Franciscan Herald Press, [1961]. 156 pp. Illus. W/o dj.

Marked "$2.95" on flyleaf.

Bulletin, 11.24.62; *Reviews*, p. 151.

237 WEIGEL, GUSTAVE, S.J. *Faith and Understanding in America.* New York: Macmillan, 1959. 170 pp. W/o dj.

Marginal linings, pp. 34, 34–35.

Bulletin, 8.22.59; *Reviews*, pp. 76–77.

238 ONG, WALTER J., S.J. *Frontiers in American Catholicism.* New York: Macmillan MP 78, 1961. 125 + viii pp. Pap.

Marginal linings on pp. 2, 3, 7, 7–8, 8, 10, 21, 22, 26, 31, 63, 102, 117, 121, 124. Marginal notation on p. 4.

Southern Cross, 3.9.63; *Reviews*, pp. 156–57.

239 AMERICAN CATHOLIC. *The American Catholic Who's Who.* Vol. 16, *1964 and 1965.* Grosse Pointe, Mich.: Walter Romig, [1965]. 505 + viii pp. W/o dj.

Added posthumously to the O'Connor library.

"O'Connor, FLANNERY, writer; *b.* Savannah, Ga., Mar. 25 '25; *dau.* Edward Francis and Regina (Cline) O.; A.B. Ga. State Coll. for Women '45, M.F.A. State U. of Ia. '48. Kenyon Review Fellow in Fiction, '53–54; O. Henry 1st prize, Ford Grant, 1960; O. Henry 1st prize, 1963. Author: *Wise Blood* ('52), *A Good Man is Hard to Find* ('55), *Violent Bear It Away* ('60). H: Milledgeville, Ga." (p. 339; col. 1).

240 BULFINCH, THOMAS. *Bulfinch's Mythology: The Age of Fable, The Age of Chivalry,* and *Legends of Charlemagne.* New York: Modern Library G14, [1934]. 778 + xi pp. Illus.

241 ELIADE, MIRCEA. *Patterns in Comparative Religion.* Trans. Rosemary Sheed. New York: Sheed and Ward, 1958; *Traité d'histoire des Religions* (Paris, n.d.). 484 + xv pp.

Marginal linings on pp. 7, 11, 14, 18, 29, 31, 38. Underlinings on pp. 13, 19, 29, 39. Marginalia: "the grotesque is naturally the bearer of mystery, is dangerous," p. 14.

"But it is quite certain that anything man has ever handled, felt, come in contact with or loved *can* become a hierophany. We know, for instance, that all the gestures, dances and games children have, and many of their toys, have a religious origin—they were once the gestures and objects of worship" (marginal lining, p. 11).

"A thing becomes sacred in so far as it embodies (that is, reveals) something other than itself" (underlining, p. 13).

"Perfection in any sphere is frightening, and this sacred or magic quality of perfection may provide an explanation for the fear that even the most civilized societies seem to feel when faced with a genius or a saint. Perfection is not of this world. It is something different, it comes from somewhere else.

"This same fear, this same scrupulous reserve, applies to everything alien, strange, new—that such astonishing things should be present is the sign of a force that, however much it is to be venerated, may be dangerous. In the Celebes, 'if the fruit of the banana appears, not at the end of the stalk but in the middle, it is *measa.* . . .' People usually say that it entails the death of its owner" (marginal lining, with annotation, p. 14).

"This setting-apart sometimes has positive effects; it does not merely isolate, it elevates. Thus ugliness and deformities, while marking out those who possess them, at the same time make them sacred. So, among the Ojibwa Indians, 'many receive the name of witches without making any pretension to the art, merely because they are deformed or ill-looking' " (marginal lining, p. 18).

"The unknown and the extraordinary are disturbing epiphanies: they indicate the presence of something *other* than the natural; the presence, or at least the call of that something" (underlining, p. 19).

". . . note first, that the religious life of the 'primitive' spreads beyond the sphere one normally allots to religious experience and theory, and second, that that religious life is always complex—the simple and one-dimensional presentation so often to be found in works of synthesis and popularization depends entirely on the author's more or less arbitrary selectiveness. Certainly some forms will be found to dominate the religious picture (totemism in Australia, for example, *mana* in Melanesia, ancestor-worship in Africa, and so on), but they are never the whole of it" (marginal lining, p. 31).

"Indeed one of the major differences separating the people of the early cultures from people to-day is precisely the utter incapacity of the latter to live their organic life (particularly as regards sex and nutrition) as a sacrament. . . . For the modern they are simply physiological acts, whereas for primitive man they were sacraments, ceremonies by means of which he communicated with the *force* which stood for Life itself" (marginal linings, p. 31).

"To the primitive, nature is never purely 'natural.' The phrase 'contemplating the vault of heaven' really means something when it is applied to primitive man, receptive to the miracles of every day to an extent we find it hard to imagine" (marginal lining, p. 38).

"Let me repeat: even before any religious values have been set upon the sky it reveals its transcendence" (underlining, p. 39).

Bulletin, 7.12.58; *Reviews*, p. 58.

242 *The Bridge: A Yearbook of Judaeo-Christian Studies*. Ed. John W. Oesterreicher. Vol. 1. New York: Pantheon, [1955]. 349 pp.

Marginal linings on pp. 65, 329, 336.

"Devout Israelites were certain that, as God had nourished their fathers with bread from heaven in the desert, so He would nourish them with heavenly food in the 'last days'; they were certain that the manna would reappear in messianic times" (marginal lining, p. 65; from Barnabas M. Ahern, C.P., "The Exodus, Then and Now").

"Now, many centuries ago, that incorrigible, 'intellectual,' Aristotle, distinguished two kinds of self-love. There is, first, self-love in the sense of loving myself as an individual, loving the *I* as against the *you;* and this, naturally, Aristotle condemned. There is, second, self-love in the sense of loving the nature that is in me: the magnificent light of intellect, the free power of will, the promise of greatness that is human nature—a God-given, God-directed, greatness, the believer would add. This kind of self-love is, as Aristotle pointed out, the very basis of love of others. If I love myself for the sake of the nature that is in me, then for precisely the same reason I must love you, also, who share that nature. Aristotle's analysis here rivals at the very least Martin Buber's much later analysis of the I-Thou relation. For what Aristotle proposes is an I-I relation: that is, the intuition that each man is 'I' and that love means the 'I' that is he and the 'I' that is I are a 'we.' The phrase 'other I' which is, superficially, a hopeless contradiction is in fact a deep truth once we have understood not the 'you-ness' of you as in Buber but the 'I-ness' of you. This kind of self-love—the love of the human person as such, and therefore quite as much in myself as in you—is high virtue, not sin" (marginal lining, p. 329; from James V. Mullaneyon in *Judaism and Modern Man* by Will Herberg).

"Here we have the most exact summation one could possibly find of why Christ is a stumbling block to so many today—their repudiation of the flesh. For no matter how often Gollancz may say that 'to part with a Christ of our own flesh and blood would be grievous,' he has nevertheless arrestingly summed up man's revulsion against the immortality of the body as an 'overestimation of the body.' That the *flesh* should be immortal is an offensive thought to many moderns. And yet those who have this revulsion against the immortality of the flesh are the ones most impassioned about the flesh of Mother Nature. Gollancz, who finds the Resurrection an 'overestimation of the body,' sings the praises of nature: 'All physical things are sacraments, and the world is so beautiful because it is a sacrament of the Supreme Beauty' " (marginal lining, p. 336).

Letters, pp. 126–27, 144, 149.

243 GUTHRIE, W.K.C. *The Greeks and Their Gods.* Boston: Beacon Press BP2, 1955 (Boston, 1950, 1954). 387 + xiv pp. Pap.

244 PORTER, KATHERINE Anne. *A Defense of Circe.* New York: Harcourt, Brace, 1955. 22 pp.

"This first edition is limited to 1700 copies privately printed for the friends of the author and her publishers as a New Year's greeting."

245 LUBAC, HENRI DE, S.J. *Aspects of Buddhism.* Trans. George Lamb. New York: Sheed and Ward, 1954. 192 + xiii pp.

Marginal linings on p. 129.

246 GRAHAM, DOM AELRED. *Zen Catholicism: A Suggestion.* New York: Harcourt, Brace and World, [1963]. 228 + xxv pp.

Signed, dated 1963. O'Connor's numbers on back dj: "17 18 32 39 45 56 84 108 *128 134 139* 157 *192*"; pp. 134 and 139 double-underlined. Marginal linings on pp. 32, 39, 40, 45, 84, 85, 103, 108, 128, 130, 134, 139, 155, 157, 191, 192. Brackets on pp. 17, 18, 20. S signs on pp. 56, 79, 118. Check marks on pp. 103, 105, 119.

"The word Zen, as we have already remarked, means 'meditation'; but Zen itself is indefinable. Echoing Confucious's cry—'I wish never to speak'—the Zen masters are fond of quoting the Buddhist dictum: *'Those who say do not know; those who know do not say.'* Nevertheless, an astonishing amount has in fact been said. What is of interest from the Christian standpoint is that Zen is not a theology; it has nothing to tell us about a supernatural revelation, nothing therefore that needs to be 'corrected' " (last sentence has marginal lining, p. 18).

"To dispose oneself to look directly at reality is, in fact, what Zen is all about" (marginal lining, p. 45).

"Once more there is unanimity among those qualified to instruct us: the Buddhist 'emptiness,' the Zen 'no-mind,' the 'void' of St. John of the Cross, the 'cloud of unknowing,' are various descriptions of the same prerequisite: to see things in their 'suchness'—above all, to bring the mind into contact with the ultimate Source of all things—one must keep one's own thoughts out of the way" (marked by an S sign, p. 79).

". . . as St. Thomas had expressed it more formally: 'In matters of Divinity, negative statements are to be preferred to positive, on account of our insufficiency, as Dionysius says' " (marginal lining, p. 191).

Review unpublished; *Reviews*, pp. 170–71; *Letters*, pp. 519, 550.

247 WOOD, ERNEST. *Zen Dictionary*. New York: Philosophical Library, [1962]. 165 pp.

Signed, dated 1963. "Publication Date November 7, 1962," printed on flyleaf; hand unknown.

Review unpublished; *Reviews*, pp. 170–71.

248 KEELER, CLYDE E. *Secrets of the Cuna Earthmother: A Comparative Study of Ancient Religions*. Exposition-University Book. New York: Exposition Press, [1960]. 352 pp. Illus.

"To Flannery O'Connor with best wishes. Clyde Keeler Jan. 27, 1960" on flyleaf. Keeler was a professor of biology at Georgia State College for Women.

249 MISSAL. DOYLE, LEONARD J., ED. *Parish Holy Week Missal*. Collegeville, Minn.: Doyle and Finegan, 1956. 192 pp. Pap. Pamphlet. In Latin and English.

This book is stored separately in the O'Connor Room with the journals and magazines.

Signed on front cover.

Social Sciences

250 McLUHAN, HERBERT MARSHALL. *The Mechanical Bride: Folk-lore of Industrial Man.* New York: Vanguard Press, [1951]. 157 + vii pp.
   Signed, dated 1954.
   Letters, pp. 173–74.

251 KIRK, RUSSELL. *Beyond the Dreams of Avarice: Essays of a Social Critic.* Chicago: Henry Regnery, 1956. 339 + x pp.
   O'Connor's numbers on back dj: "56 80 139 90." Marginal linings on pp. 12, 48, 56, 80, 83, 90, 139, 176, 177. Check marks on pp. viii, 11. Marginalia: "W. C. Brownell said this first—" against bracketed passage, p. 7; "Brownell again," against lined passage on p. 78.
   Bulletin, 7.21.56; *Reviews,* p. 23; *Letters,* p. 161.

252 ———. *The Conservative Mind: From Burke to Santayana.* Chicago: Henry Regnery, 1953 (Chicago, 1953). 458 pp.
   Signed, dated 1954. Marginal linings on pp. 59, 141, 249. Brackets, p. 27.
   "Abstract sentimentality ends in real brutality" (marginal lining, p. 141).
   Letters, pp. 110, 161.

253 PICARD, MAX. *Hitler in Our Selves.* Trans. Heinrich Hauser. Introduction by Robert S. Hartman. Hinsdale, Ill.: Henry Regnery, 1947. 272 pp.

254 CURTIS, EDITH ROELKER. *A Season in Utopia: The Story of Brook Farm.* New York: Thomas Nelson and Sons, [1961]. 346 pp.
   Signed, dated 1963. "14 72" written on front jacket cover.

255 TOCQUEVILLE, ALEXIS DE. *Democracy in America.* Revised by Francis Bowen. Ed. and corrected, with a historical essay, notes, and bibliographies, by Phillips Bradley. Vol. 1. New York: Vintage K-5A, 1954 (New York, 1945). 452 + xvi + xi pp. Pap.

Henry Reeve text.

Signed "F. O'Connor 1954" on flyleaf. Marginal linings on pp. 235, 410, 443, 452. Marginalia: question mark on p. 410.

"Besides, what is to be feared is not so much the immorality of the great as the fact that immorality may lead to greatness" (marginal lining, p. 235).

256 ———. *Democracy in America.* Vol. 2. New York: Vintage K-5B, 1954 (New York, 1945). 518 + xii pp. Pap.

Signed "F. O'Connor 1954" on flyleaf. Marginal notes on pp. 4, 18, 45, 48, 53, 69, 80, 88, 92, 93, 124, 132, 134, 228. Underlinings on p. 4. Marginalia: "real?" p. 75.

"America is therefore one of the countries where the precepts of Descartes are least studied and are best applied" (marginal notation, p. 4).

"Thus they fall to denying what they cannot comprehend; which leaves them but little faith for whatever is extraordinary and an almost insurmountable distaste for whatever is supernatural" (underlining, p. 4).

"It may be foreseen in like manner that poets living in democratic times will prefer the delineation of passions and ideas to that of persons and achievements. The language, the dress, and the daily actions of men in democracies are repugnant to conceptions of the ideal. These things are not poetical in themselves; and if it were otherwise, they would cease to be so, because they are too familiar to all those to whom the poet would speak of them. This forces the poet constantly to search below the external surface which is palpable to the senses, in order to read the inner soul; and nothing lends itself more to the delineation of the ideal than the scrutiny of the hidden depths in the immaterial nature of man. I need not traverse earth and sky to discover a wondrous object woven of contrasts, of infinite greatness and littleness, of intense gloom and amazing brightness, capable at once of exciting pity, admiration, terror, contempt. I have only to look at myself. Man springs out of nothing, crosses time, and disappears forever in the bosom of God; he is seen but for a moment, wandering on the verge of the two abysses, and there he is lost" (marginal lining, p. 80).

" 'To be mistaken in believing that the Christian religion is true,' says Pascal, 'is no great loss to anyone; but how dreadful to be mistaken in believing it to be false' " (marginal lining, p. 134).

257 KERR, WALTER. *Criticism and Censorship.* Milwaukee: Bruce Publishing, 1957 (Milwaukee, 1954). 86 + vi pp. Pap.

The Gabriel Richard Lecture. Cosponsored by the National Catholic Educational Association and Trinity College, Washington, D.C.

Signed "F. O'Connor" on front cover. Marginal lining on pp. 44, 54, 55, 85. Correction of text, p. 56.

Bulletin, 3.2.57; *Reviews,* pp. 36–37; *Letters,* p. 218.

258 DRUCKER, PETER F. *The New Society: The Anatomy of the Industrial Order.* New York: Harper and Brothers, [1950]. 356 + ix pp.

Signed, dated 1955. Marginal linings on pp. 3, 6.

259 THOMAS AQUINAS, SAINT. *Treatise on Law, On Truth and Falsity,* and *On Human Knowledge* (*Summa Theologica,* questions 90–97; part 1, questions 16–17; questions 84–88). Gateway Edition 6032. Chicago: Henry Regnery, n.d. 244 + x pp. Pap.

Introduction to *Treatise on Law* by Stanley Parry.

260 AVALOS, BEATRICE. *New Men for New Times: A Christian Philosophy of Education.* New York: Sheed and Ward, [1962]. 182 pp.

Marginal lining on p. 27.

Southern Cross, 3.16.63, p. 2; *Reviews,* pp. 157–59.

261 YEATS, W. B. *Mythologies.* New York: Macmillan, 1959. [369] + vii pp.

Signed, dated 1959.

Language

262 PARTRIDGE, ERIC. *Origins: A Short Etymological Dictionary of Modern English.* New York: Macmillan, 1959 (New York, 1958). 970 + xix pp.

263 WEBSTER. *Webster's New International Dictionary of the English Language.* Springfield, Mass.: G. and C. Merriam, 1925. 2,620 + cxi + 256 pp. Illus. Maps. Thumb indexed. Oversize. Loose binding.

Based on the International Dictionary of 1890 and 1900, completely revised, with a reference history of the world. W. T. Harris, editor in chief. F. Sturges Allen, general editor.

Verso of flyleaf reads, "Property of T. J. Lyon."

Pure Sciences

264 BARNETT, LINCOLN. *The Universe and Dr. Einstein.* Foreword by Albert Einstein. New York: New American Library, Mentor MD231, 1960 [New York, 1948]. 128 pp. Pap. Illus.

On verso of dedication page: "Flannery—Pax Vacum! Roslyn 12-25-61."

265 UNITED STATES DEPARTMENT OF AGRICULTURE. *Water: The Yearbook of Agriculture 1955.* Foreword by Ezra Taft Benson, secretary of agriculture. Preface by Alfred Stefferud, editor. 84th Cong., 1st sess., House Document no. 32. Washington, D.C.: U.S. Dept. of Agriculture, 1955. 751 + xiii pp. Illus. W/o dj.

Probably added posthumously.

Applied Sciences

266 JENCKS, BARBARA C. *The Dr. Tom Dooley Story.* Famous Catholic American Series, no. 1. South Bend, Ind.: McClave Printing, 1961. 2d printing. 16 pp. Pamphlet. Pap.

On inside front cover: "To Flannery O'Connor, whom

I've long admired and hope someday to meet—Tom was 'a good man—hard to find.' Barbara C. Jencks."

267 FREUD, SIGMUND. *The Basic Writings of Sigmund Freud*. Trans. and ed., with an introduction, by A. A. Brill. New York: Modern Library G39, 1938. 1001 + vi pp. W/o dj.

Includes *Psychopathology of Everyday Life* (pp. 33–178); *The Interpretation of Dreams* (pp. 179–549); *Three Contributions to the Theory of Sex* (pp. 551–629); *Wit and Its Relation to the Unconscious* (pp. 631–803); *Totem and Taboo* (pp. 805–930); and *The History of the Psychoanalytic Movement* (pp. 931–77).

Signed, dated 1947. Marginal lining on p. 193. Underlining on p. 193. Check marks, p. 193.

"Regarded in isolation, an idea may be quite insignificant, and venturesome in the extreme, but it may acquire importance from an idea which follows it; perhaps, in a certain collocation with other ideas, which may seem equally absurd, it may be capable of furnishing a very serviceable link. The intellect cannot judge all these ideas unless it can retain them until it has considered them in connection with these other ideas. In the case of a creative mind, it seems to me, the intellect has withdrawn its watchers from the gates, and the ideas rush in pell-mell, and only then does it review and inspect the multitude" (first sentence underlined; remainder marked by marginal lining, p. 193).

268 JUNG, C. G. *Modern Man in Search of a Soul*. Trans. W. S. Dell and Cary F. Baynes. Preface by Baynes. New York: Harcourt, Brace, Harvest HB2, [1957], (1933). 244 + ix pp. Pap.

Marginal linings on pp. 34, 35, 61, 122, 126, 143, 145, 168, 169, 170–71, 171, 172, 194, 198, 225, 235. Underlinings on pp. 117, 168, 194, 196–97, 197, 198, 211, 212, 214, 226, 234.

". . . what is inferior or even worthless belongs to me as my shadow and gives me substance and mass. How can I be substantial if I fail to cast a shadow? I must have a dark side also if I am to be whole; and inasmuch as I become conscious of my shadow I also remember that I am a human being like any other" (marginal lining, p. 35).

"About a third of my cases are suffering from no clinically definable neurosis, but from the senselessness and emptiness of their lives. It seems to me, however, that this can well be described as the general neurosis of our time. Fully two-thirds of my patients have passed middle age.

"It is difficult to treat patients of this particular kind by rational methods, because they are in the main socially well-adapted individuals of considerable ability, to whom normalization means nothing" (marginal lining, p. 61).

" 'The strange thing is that man will not learn that God is his father.' That is what Freud would never learn, and what all those who share his outlook forbid themselves to learn. At least, they never find the key to this knowledge. Theology does not help those who are looking for the key, because theology demands faith, and faith cannot be made: it is in the truest sense a gift of grace. We moderns are faced with the necessity of rediscovering the life of the spirit; we must experience it anew for ourselves. It is the only way in which we can break the spell that binds us to the cycle of biological events" (marginal lining, p. 122).

". . . civilized man of today shows these archaic processes as well, and not merely in the form of sporadic 'throwbacks' from the level of modern social life. On the contrary, every civilized human being, whatever his conscious development, is still an archaic man at the deeper levels of his psyche. Just as the human body connects us with the mammals and displays numerous relics of earlier evolutionary stages going back even to the reptilian age, so the human psyche is likewise a product of evolution which, when followed up to its origins, shows countless archaic traits" (marginal lining, p. 126).

"In the primitive world everything has psychic qualities. Everything is endowed with the elements of man's psyche—

or let us say, of the human psyche, of the collective unconscious, for there is as yet no individual psychic life. Let us not
forget, in this connection, that what the Christian sacrament
of baptism purports to do is of the greatest importance for the
psychic development of mankind. Baptism endows the human being with a unique soul. I do not mean, of course, the
baptismal rite in itself as a magical act that is effective at one
performance. I mean that the idea of baptism lifts a man out
of his archaic identification with the world and changes him
into a being who stands above it. The fact that mankind has
risen to the level of this idea is baptism in the deepest sense,
for it means the birth of spiritual man who transcends nature" (marginal lining, p. 145).

"What is essential in a work of art is that it should rise far
above the realm of personal life and speak from the spirit
and heart of the poet as man to the spirit and heart of
mankind. The personal aspect is a limitation—and even a
sin—in the realm of art. When a form of 'art' is primarily
personal it deserves to be treated as if it were a neurosis"
(marginal lining, last two sentences also underlined,
p. 168).

"Art is a kind of innate drive that seizes a human being and
makes him its instrument. The artist is not a person endowed
with free will who seeks his own ends, but one who allows
art to realize its purposes through him. As a human being he
may have moods and a will and personal aims, but as an
artist he is 'man' in a higher sense—he is 'collective man'—
one who carries and shapes the unconscious, psychic life of
mankind" (marginal lining, p. 169).

"Whenever the creative force predominates, human life
is ruled and molded by the unconscious as against the active will, and the conscious ego is swept along on a subter-
ranean current, being nothing more than a helpless ob-
server of events. The work in process becomes the poet's
fate and determines his psychic development. It is not

Goethe who creates *Faust*, but *Faust* which creates Goethe. And what is *Faust* but a symbol? By this I do not mean an allegory that points to something all too familiar, but an expression that stands for something not clearly known and yet profoundly alive. Here it is something that lives in the soul of every German, and that Goethe has helped to bring to birth" (marginal lining, pp. 170–71).

"He [the poet] has done the best that in him lies in giving it form, and he must leave the interpretation to others and to the future. A great work of art is like a dream; for all its apparent obviousness it does not explain itself and is never unequivocal. A dream never says: 'You ought,' or: 'This is the truth.' It presents an image in much the same way as nature allows a plant to grow, and we must draw our own conclusions" (marginal lining, p. 171).

"The man whom we can with justice call 'modern' is solitary" (underlining, p. 197).

"An honest profession of modernity means voluntarily declaring bankruptcy, taking the vows of poverty and chastity in a new sense, and—what is still more painful—renouncing the halo which history bestows as a mark of its sanction. To be 'unhistorical' is the Promethean sin, and in this sense modern man lives in sin. A higher level of consciousness is like a burden of guilt. But, as I have said, only the man who has outgrown the stages of consciousness belonging to the past and has amply fulfilled the duties appointed for him by his world, can achieve a full consciousness of the present. To do this he must be sound and proficient in the best sense—a man who has achieved as much as other people, and even a little more. It is these qualities which enable him to gain the next highest level of consciousness" (marginal lining, p. 198).

"And it is just people of the lower social levels who follow the unconscious forces of the psyche; it is the much-derided, silent folk of the land—those who are less infected with academic prejudices than great celebrities are wont to be. All these people, looked at from above, present mostly a dreary or laughable comedy; and yet they are as impressively simple as those Galileans who were once called blessed" (underlining, p. 211).

"The unexpected result of this spiritual change is that an uglier face is put upon the world. It becomes so ugly that no one can love it any longer—we cannot even love ourselves—and in the end there is nothing in the outer world to draw us away from the reality of the life within" (underlining, p. 212).

"Everyday reasonableness, sound human judgement, and science as a compendium of common sense, certainly help us over a good part of the road; yet they do not go beyond that frontier of human life which surrounds the commonplace and matter-of-fact, the merely average and normal. They afford, after all, no answer to the question of spiritual suffering and its innermost meaning. A psycho-neurosis must be understood as the suffering of a human being who has not discovered what life means for him. But all creativeness in the realm of the spirit as well as every psychic advance of man arises from a state of mental suffering, and it is spiritual stagnation, psychic sterility, which causes this state.

"The doctor who realizes this truth sees a territory opened before him which he approaches with the greatest hesitation. He is now confronted with the necessity of conveying to his patient the healing fiction, the meaning that quickens—for it is this that the patient longs for, over and above all that reason and science can give him. The patient is looking for something that will take possession of him and give meaning and form to the confusion of his neurotic mind" (marginal lining, p. 225).

"The way to experience, moreover, is anything but a clever trick; it is rather a venture which requires us to commit ourselves with our whole being" (underlined, p. 226).

"What I do unto the least of my brethren, that I do unto Christ. But what if I should discover that the least amongst them all, the poorest of all the beggars, the most impudent of all the offenders, the very enemy himself—that these are within me, and that I myself stand in need of the alms of my own kindness—that I myself am the enemy who must be loved—what then? As a rule, the Christian's attitude is then reversed; there is no longer any question of love or long-suffering; we say to the brother within us 'Raca,' and condemn and rage against ourselves. We hide it from the world; we refuse to admit ever having met this least among the lowly in ourselves. Had it been God himself who drew near to us in this despicable form, we should have denied him a thousand times before a single cock had crowed" (marginal lining, p. 235).

Letters, pp. 103, 382–83, 387–88, 491.

The Arts

269 MALRAUX, ANDRÉ. *The Voices of Silence.* Trans. Stuart Gilbert. Garden City, N.Y.: Doubleday, 1953; *Les Voix du Silence* (Paris, 1953). 661 pp. Illus. Boxed.

   Marginalia: "348" on p. 312; "p. 312" on p. 348.

   Letters, pp. 372, 494, 498.

270 BERENSON, BERNARD. *Aesthetics and History.* Garden City, N.Y.: Doubleday, Anchor A36, [1953]; [New York, 1948]. 283 pp. Pap.

271 CARRITT, E. F., ED. *Philosophies of Beauty: From Socrates to Robert Bridges, Being the Sources of Aesthetic Theory.* Foreword by D. W. Prall. New York: Oxford University Press, 1931. 334 + xxix pp. W/o dj.

   Anthology of selections by Carritt.

   Signed "Flannery O'Connor Milledgeville, Georgia" (handwriting seems earlier than usual). Marginal lining on p. 207. Underlinings on pp. 131, 134, 207, 236, 237, 238, 239–40, 240, 241. Check mark on p. 131. Marginalia: "mod-

ern art produces the nature of things" (notation to Plato's
Republic), p. 21; "Croce" (to Kant), p. 114; "Croce there,"
"Croce here," "theoretical" (all to Coleridge), p. 134;
"Proust" (to Bergson), p. 207; "art individual," "comedy
type" (both to Bergson), p. 208.

"Beneath the thousand rudimentary actions which are
the outward and visible signs of an emotion, behind the
commonplace, conventional expression that both reveals
and conceals an individual mental state, it is the emotion,
the original mood, to which they attain in its undefiled
essence. And then, to induce us to make the same effort
ourselves, they contrive to make us see something of what
they have seen: by rhythmical arrangement of words,
which thus become organized and animated with a life of
their own, they tell us—or rather suggest—things that
speech was not calculated to express. Others delve yet
deeper still. Beneath these joys and sorrows which can, at a
pinch, be translated into language, they grasp something
that has nothing in common with language, certain
rhythms of life and breath that are closer to man than his
inmost feelings" (from Bergson; marginal lining, p. 207).

". . . realism is in the work when idealism is in the soul,
and that it is only through ideality that we can resume
contact with reality" (from Bergson; underlining, p. 207).

"And since it is not produced by an act of will, art is
exempt from moral distinctions" (from Croce; underlining,
p. 236).

"As a man he [the artist] comes under its laws and never
escapes the duties of a man. His art itself, that art which is
not and cannot be morality, he must consider as a mission,
to be exercised as if it were a priesthood" (from Croce;
underlining, p. 237).

". . . ideality is the very essence of art. No sooner are
reflections and judgement developed out of this ideality
than art fades and dies. It dies in the artist, who becomes a

critic; and it dies in his audience, who become critics of life
instead of his enchanted listeners" (from Croce; underlining, p. 239).

"Intuition is truly artistic, is truly intuition, and not a
chaotic mass of images, only when it is animated by a vital
principle native to itself" (from Croce; underlining, p. 240).

"What gives unity and coherence to intuition is feeling"
(from Croce; underlining, p. 241).

272 MARITAIN, JACQUES. *Art and Scholasticism: With Other Essays*
(*Art et Scolastique*). Trans. J. F. Scanlan. New York: Charles
Scribner's Sons, [1930]. 177 + ix pp.

Signed. Marginal linings on pp. 1, 6, 8, 9, 10, 12, 13, 20,
21, 54, 55, 58, 59. Underlining on pp. 6, 20. Check marks on
pp. 11, 21. Arrow, p. 6. Question mark, p. 13.

"As opposed to Action, the Schoolmen defined Making
as *productive action*, considered not in relation to the use to
which, assuming it, we put our freedom, but simply *in
relation to the thing produced* or the work taken by itself. This
action is what it ought to be, is good of its kind, if it con-
forms to the rules and the end peculiar to the work to be
produced; and the result to which it is directed, if it is good,
is for the work in question to be good in itself. So Making is
ordered to such-and-such a definite end, separate and self-
sufficient, not to the common end of human life; and it
relates to the peculiar good or perfection not of the man
making, but of the work made" (paragraph partly margi-
nally lined, partly underlined, p. 6).

"The truth is that such conflicts can be abolished only on
condition that a deep humility make the artist as it were
unconscious of his art, or if the all-powerful function of
wisdom imbue everything in him with the repose and peace
of love. Fra Angelico felt no such inner vexation of spirit"
(double marginal lining, p. 12).

". . . their innermost being, their spiritual essence, their
operative mystery, is above all the peculiar principle of intel-

ligibility, the peculiar *clarity* of every thing. Every form, more-over, is a remnant or a ray of the creative Mind impressed upon the heart of the being created. All order and propor-tion, on the other hand, are the work of the mind. So, to say with the Schoolmen that beauty is the *splendour of form shin-ing on the proportioned parts of matter* is to say that it is a light-ning of mind on a matter intelligently arranged. The mind rejoices in the beautiful because in the beautiful it finds itself again: recognizes itself, and comes into contact with its very own light. This is so true that they especially perceive and particularly relish the beauty of things who, like St. Francis of Assisi, for example, know that they emanate from a mind and refer them to their Author" (marginal lining, p. 20).

"The mind, then, spared the least effort of abstraction, rejoices without labour and without discussion. It is ex-cused its customary task, it has not to extricate something intelligible from the matter in which it is buried and then step by step go through its various attributes" (four mar-ginal linings, p. 21).

"Do not make the absurd attempt to sever in yourself the artist and the Christian. They are one, if you really *are* a Christian, and if your art is not isolated from your soul by some aesthetic system. But apply only the artist in you to the work in hand; precisely because they are one, the work will be as wholly of the one as of the other" (marginal lining, p. 54).

Letters, pp. xvii, 42, 47, 144, 157, 214, 216, 221.

273 ORTEGA Y GASSET, JOSÉ. *The Dehumanization of Art and Other Writings on Art and Culture.* Trans. Willard R. Trask. Garden City, N.Y.: Doubleday, Anchor A72, 1956. 187 pp. Pap.

274 PEPPER, STEPHEN C. *The Basis of Criticism in the Arts.* Preface and introduction by Pepper. Cambridge: Harvard Univer-sity Press, 1946 [1945]. 177 + viii pp. W/o dj.

Signed, dated October 1946. Marginal linings on pp. 7, 52, 65. Underlinings on pp. 4, 6, 52, 65, 68, 69, 71, 74, 81, 83,

89, 98, 101, 102, 103, 105, 112, 146, 148, 149, 156–57, 164, 166, 170, 171. Check marks on pp. 23, 77, 89, 158. Marginalia: "Imp.," p. 31; "Croce in the woodpile," p. 87; "therefore not mutually exclusive with the mechanist distinction of art and non art," p. 105; "differing in kind as well as degree," p. 157. Question mark on pp. 156, 166.

"Structural corroboration is the corroboration of fact with fact. It is not a multiplicity of observations of one identical fact, but an observed convergence of many different facts towards one result. We have a crude use of it in what we call circumstantial evidence, where a variety of different circumstances all point to a single conclusion" (marginal lining, p. 7).

"Nothing has less to do with the real merit of a work of imagination than the capacity of all men to appreciate it; the true test is the degree and kind of satisfaction it can give to him who appreciates it most" (quoting Santayana; underlining, p. 52).

The critic "is to judge the degree of realization of experience achieved by an artist—the vividness and the spread of it. He will consider whether the artist has made the most of his emotional material, or has gone beyond the limits of aesthetic endurance and destroyed aesthetic distance. He will show the relation of the work to its social context. He will consider the suitability of the structure of the work. And for the benefit of the spectator he will analyze the structure and exhibit its details, so that these will not be missed and may be funded in the full realization of the work in its total fused quality" (underlined, p. 68).

"The perception of a work of art is clearly the awareness of the quality of a situation" (underlining, p. 69).

". . . the aesthetic work of art is the cumulative succession of intermittent perceptions" (underlining, p. 71).

"The only adequate judgment of a work of art, therefore, is one based on the fullest realization of it, on a perception which contains the funded experiences of many preceding perceptions" (underlining, p. 71).

"Organicism proposes a justification for a final objective judgment for a highly integrated work of art" (marginal lining, p. 81).

"The aesthetic value of a work of art as an integration of feeling is as independent of any artist's subjective idea of what he wanted to do when he was making it, as the cognitive value of a scientific description of fact is independent of a scientist's idea of what he wanted to find when he started observing" (underlining, p. 83).

"The aesthetic materials seek their own satisfying structure and equilibrium through the artist, who does not dictate but follows their guidance" (underlining, p. 83).

"The perceptual judgment and the judgment of value at this level of criticism accordingly merge and mutually affect each other" (underlining, p. 171).

275 Leeuw, Gerardus van der. *Sacred and Profane Beauty: The Holy in Art.* Trans. David E. Green. Preface by Mircea Eliade. New York: Holt, Rinehart and Winston, [1963]; *Vom Heiligen in der Kunst* (n.p., 1932). 357 + xx pp.

Signed, dated 1963. Marginal lining on p. 33.

"The great difficulty, indeed the tragedy of our modern life, lies in the fact that we differentiate between the things which concern us and things which do not concern us" (marginal lining, p. 33).

276 Our Lady. *Our Lady in Art.* Vol. 1. Annotations and descriptions by the Right Rev. David T. O'Dwyer. Washington, D.C.: Salve Regina Press, [1934]. [64] pp. Illus. W/o dj.

Signed "Mary Flannery O'Connor August 1934" on flyleaf.

277 Sypher, Wylie. *Four Stages of Renaissance Style: Transformations in Art and Literature, 1400–1700.* Garden City, N.Y.: Doubleday, Anchor A45, 1955. 312 pp. Pap. Illus.

278 Lewis, Wyndham. *The Demon of Progress in the Arts.* Chicago: Henry Regnery, 1955. 97 + vi pp. Plates.

Letters, p. 161.

279 JACKSON, HOLBROOK. *The Eighteen Nineties: A Review of Art and Ideas at the Close of the Nineteenth Century*. Harmondsworth, England: Penguin, Pelican A58, 1950 (1913). 317 pp. Pap.

Marginal linings on pp. 51, 59. Check mark on pp. 62, 115.

280 WRIGHT, CLIFFORD. *Helten i den nye verden: 12 kapitler om amerikansk kunst—fra en kunstners synspunkt* (Hero in the New World: Twelve Chapters About American Art). Copenhagen: Borgens Forlag, 1963. 80 pp. Pap. Plates. In Norwegian.

All pages uncut.

"To Flannery with affectionate regards, Clifford Oct. 29, 1963" on flyleaf.

281 ADAMS, HENRY. *Mont-Saint-Michel and Chartres*. Introduction by Ralph Adams Cram. Garden City, N.Y.: Doubleday, Anchor A166, 1959. 455 + xvi pp. Pap. Illus.

282 DAUMIER, HONORÉ. JAMES, HENRY. *Daumier: Caricaturist*. Miniature Books. Emmaus, Pa.: Rodale Press, 1954. [36] pp. Illus. Plasticine wrap.

Letters, p. 494.

283 BEERBOHM, MAX. *Max's Nineties: Drawings, 1892–1899*. Introduction by Osbert Lancaster. Philadelphia: J. B. Lippincott, 1958. [56] pp. Drawings.

284 LEAR, EDWARD. *Teapots and Quails and Other New Nonsenses*. Ed. Angus Davidson and Philip Hofer. Introduction by Davidson. Foreword by Hofer. London: John Murray, 1954 (1953). [64] pp. Illus.

285 CAPOTE, TRUMAN. *The Muses Are Heard*. New York: Modern Library P35, [1956]. 182 pp. Pap.

Signed on inside front cover.

Letters, p. 368.

286 LYNCH, WILLIAM F., S.J. *The Image Industries*. New York: Sheed and Ward, [1959]. 159 pp.

Signed, dated 1959. O'Connor's note on front dj: "15 24

27 38 40 80 126 142." Marginal linings on pp. 15, 24, 27, 38, 40, 80. Underlining on p. 15. Marginal pointing, p. 142.

"It is that kind of identification of the solemn levels of human feeling with anything and everything which produces tawdriness and stupidity. It is a form of judging which corrupts the very deepest fibres of judgment and leaves the soul open to anything and everything—except reality" (marginal lining notation, p. 27).

"The discussion should rather revolve around this point: whether or no the mass arts are creating a flat and neutral image of man that seldom in its sensibility touches the heights and the depths of reality as it is described by Christianity" (marginal lining, p. 38).

"A theology of creativity. That would be a great goal, to be accomplished only by the united efforts of many minds who would be willing to admit that the problem is crucial and who would be willing to pay the price of making themselves substantially competent in the worlds of both theology and art. There are those among us who will surely say that the net result would be neither professional theology nor professional art, and this may be true, though I am not quite sure that I should admit so much in advance. My real feeling is that this is a purely technical question which tends to hide the very important fact that religion is not only a body of revealed truth technically expressible in conceptual form but that it is also a living and moving history, always itself in creative movement and always on the way to unpredictable goals in history. It is the actual and substantive living and growing of Christ in the forms of society and history, the filling out of his body, the filling out of his sufferings. God has not placed the work, the competencies, the sensibilities of the artist outside of this movement" (indicated by marginal pointing, p. 142).

Bulletin, 8.8.59; *Reviews,* pp. 74–75.

Literature

287 LITERARY SCHOLARSHIP. FOERSTER, NORMAN, JOHN C. McGALLIARD, RENÉ WELLEK, AUSTIN WARREN, AND WILBUR L. SCHRAMM. *Literary Scholarship: Its Aims and Methods.* Chapel Hill: University of North Carolina Press, 1941. 269 + ix pp. W/o dj.

Signed, dated October, 1946. Marginal linings on pp. 96, 121. Underlinings on pp. 97, 98, 98–99, 100, 104, 107, 112, 113, 117, 118, 120, 120–21, 121, 139, 142, 143, 145, 146, 147, 148, 150, 151, 159, 162, 165, 173–74. Check mark on p. 111. Question mark on p. 120. Marginalia: "fallacious analogy?" p. 121; "formism?" p. 142; "contextualism? organicism?" p. 43; "Titian V[arga] girl," p. 148 (referring to entry 274, pp. 52–53), "intensity duration varied values," p. 155; "organicism," p. 158.

"Even Coleridge's famous distinction between fancy and imagination seems less valuable as a distinction in psychology than as an observation of two types of imagery which could be differentiated without the assumption of two distinct powers of the mind" (underlining, from Wellek, p. 104).

"The meaning of a poem, not to be drawn off in a prose paraphrase, is constituted not only by its conceptual ideas but by the rhythms, the imagery, the metaphors operating in close conjunction; and these elements must properly be studied as they interact in the organism" (underlining, from Warren, p. 143).

". . . the response to literature is not permanent withdrawal from action or aesthetic escape from life but an immediate contemplation which helps the reader to considered action instead of instinctive behavior" (from Warren; underlining, p. 150).

288 VIVAS, ELISEO. *Creation and Discovery: Essays in Criticism and Aesthetics.* New York: Noonday Press, 1955. 306 + xiv pp.

289 ELIOT, T. S. *The Sacred Wood: Essays on Poetry and Criticism.* London: Methuen, University UP-11, 1960 (London, 1920). 171 + xix pp. Pap.

290 HYMAN, STANLEY EDGAR. *The Armed Vision: A Study in the Methods of Modern Literary Criticism.* Rev. ed., abridged by Hyman. New York: Vintage, 1955 (New York, 1948). 402 + xii + xxvii pp. Pap.

Underlining on p. 130.

291 ELIOT, T. S. *On Poetry and Poets.* New York: Noonday Press N214, 1961 (1943). 308 + xii pp. Pap.

Marginal lining on p. 195.

"Nowadays we use words so loosely that a writer's meaning may sometimes be concealed from us, simply because he has said exactly what he meant" (marginal lining, p. 195).

Letters, p. 170.

292 MURRY, J. MIDDLETON. *The Problem of Style.* London: Oxford University Press, Oxford Paperbacks 11, 1961 (London, 1922). 133 + x pp. Pap.

Signed "F. O'Connor 1961." Marginal linings on pp. 47, 55, 76.

"Where a metaphor adds nothing to the precision with which a thought is expressed, then it is unnecessary and to be sacrificed without compunction" (marginal lining, p. 76).

293 STRUNK, WILLIAM, JR. *The Elements of Style.* Rev., with an introduction and added chapter, by E. B. White. New York: Macmillan, 1959. 71 + xiv pp. Pap.

Signed on front cover "Sr. Alice."

294 REHDER, JESSIE. *The Young Writer at Work.* New York: Odyssey Press, [1962]. 274 + x pp. W/o dj.

Signed "F. O'Connor 1962." Ellen Glasgow, *A Certain Measure,* checked in list of acknowledgments, p. v. "A Good Man Is Hard to Find" discussed under "Hints for Revision," pp. 218, 220 and the following pages.

295 WEST, JESSAMYN. *The Reading Public.* New York: Harcourt, Brace, 1953. 29 pp.

"This first edition of *The Reading Public* is privately printed for the friends of the author and her publishers as a New Year's greeting."

296 CASSILL, R. V. *Writing Fiction*. New York: Pocket Books, Permabook M7508, 1963 (New York, 1962). 304 + xv pp. Pap.

297 GARDNER, JOHN, AND LENNIS DUNLAP. *The Forms of Fiction*. New York: Random House, [1962]. 657 + x pp. W/o dj.

Katherine Anne Porter's "The Witness," Peter Taylor's "The Fancy Woman," and Flannery O'Connor's "A Good Man Is Hard to Find" (pp. 305–19) are checked in the table of contents, p. x.

298 INTRODUCTION. BARROWS, HERBERT, HUBERT HEFFNER, JOHN CIARDI, AND WALLACE DOUGLAS. *An Introduction to Literature: In Four Parts*. Boston: Houghton Mifflin, [1959]. 1331 + xv pp. W/o dj.

General editor, Gordon N. Ray. Contents include "Reading the Short Story" by Barrows, "The Nature of Drama" by Heffner, "How Does a Poem Mean?" by Ciardi, and "The Character of Prose" by Douglas. Anthology.

Signed, and dated 1959. "The Displaced Person," pp. 306–37; biographical introduction, pp. 305–6; discussion questions, pp. 337–38.

299 PHILLIPS, WILLIAM, AND PHILIP RAHV, EDS. *The Avon Book of Modern Writing*. New York: Avon Publications AT66, [1953]. 281 pp. Pap.

"A Good Man Is Hard to Find," pp. 186–99; biographical note, p. 280.

300 GOLLANCZ, VICTOR, ED. *From Darkness to Light: A Confession of Faith in the Form of an Anthology*. New York: Harper and Brothers, [1956]. 683 pp.

Literary passages topically arranged. O'Connor's "The Knowledge of Mercy," a paragraph from "The Artificial Nigger," p. 266. She is listed as a "contemporary American novelist," p. 637.

301 ACTS. KOZLENKO, WILLIAM, ED. *Acts of Violence.* New York: Pyramid Books G425, 1959. 192 pp. Pap.
  "A Good Man is Hard to Find," pp. 89–106.

302 BROOKS, CLEANTH, JR., AND ROBERT PENN WARREN, EDS. *Understanding Poetry: An Anthology for College Students.* New York: Henry Holt, 1945 (New York, 1938). 680 + xxiv pp. W/o dj.
  Signed. Possibly used as a text at the State University of Iowa. Underlinings on pp. 295, 413, 493. Check mark by William Blake, "London," p. 654. Marginalia: "Thurs. Read to p. 255 include Browning," p. 209; stray marking, p. 655.

303 LOWELL, ROBERT. *Imitations.* New York: Farrar, Straus and Cudahy, [1961]. 149 + xiv pp.

304 BLODGETT, HAROLD, ED. *The Story Survey.* Chicago: J. B. Lippincott, [1939], 797 + viii pp. W/o dj.
  Signed "M. F. O'Connor 305 W. Green St. Milledgeville." Probably used as a text at Georgia State College for Women. Underlinings on pp. 7, 8, 37, 427. Check marks on pp. 65, 214, 223, 384, 472, 484, 555, 644. Checked in table of contents: Henry James, "Paste"; H. C. Bunner, "The Two Churches of Quawket"; Ring Lardner, "There Are Smiles"; Conrad Aiken, "Your Obituary, Well Written"; Wilbur Daniel Steele, "How Beautiful With Shoes"; William Faulkner, "That Evening Sun"; Walter D. Edmonds, "Blind Eve" (marked "setting"); Lois Montross, "A Day in New York"; Ernest Hemingway, "After the Storm"; Ruth Suckow, "Golden Wedding"; Owen Francis, "The Ladies Call on Mr. Pussick"; Marjorie Kinnan Rawlings, "The Pardon"; Josephine Johnson, "Arcadia Recalled"; William Saroyan, "A Cold Day"; Kathleen Morehouse, "With the Fog"; Gerald Warner Brace, "Deep Water Man"; James Still, "Job's Tears"; Sherwood Anderson, "Sophistication"; Ferner Nuhn, "Ten"; Frances Newman, "Rachel and Her Children"; Edwin Granberry, "A Trip to Czardis" (marked "outside" and "understatement children"); Nancy Hale, "No One My Grief Can Tell"; Wilkie

Collins, "A Terribly Strange Bed" (marked "not"); Robert Louis Stevenson, "A Lodging for the Night" (marked "class" and starred); John Galsworthy, "Salta Pro Nobis" (marked "class" and starred); James Joyce, "A Little Cloud" (starred); D. H. Lawrence, "The Blind Man"; James Stephens, "The Horses" (starred); A. E. Coppard, "The Handsome Lady"; Walter de la Mare, "The Nap" (starred); Sheila Kaye-Smith, "The Mockbeggar" (marked "not"); Seán O'Faoláin, "Lonely Lives"; Honoré de Balzac, "A Passion in the Desert"; Alphonse Daudet, "M. Seguin's Goat"; Guy de Maupassant, "Two Friends" (marked "take"); Anatole France, "The Manuscript of a Village Doctor" (marked "take" and starred); August Strindberg, "Autumn" (marked "take"); Theodor Storm, "Veronika" (marked "take"); Thomas Mann, "The Hungry"; Anton Chekhov, "Grief" (marked "take" and starred); Ivan S. Turgenev, "The District Doctor" (marked "take" and starred); Maxim Gorky, "One Autumn Night" (starred); S. Sergeev-Tzensky, "The Man You Couldn't Kill"; Luigi Pirandello, "The House of Agony"; Ignazio Silone, "The Trap." Other marginalia: "America France England Russia," p. ix; "read," p. 7; "legendised short story—tells as if it were a yarn told to him—used old motifs & legends—made them ridiculous—took horror away" (on Washington Irving, p. 37); "style," p. 37; "weaknesses (1) allegorization makes unreality (2) lacks broad intellectual range (3) lacked broad interest in people" (on Hawthorne), p. 43; "not enough characterization definitely romanticist in writing gothic—not romantic because no interest in reform, humanitarianism new interpretation of nature, exploration of the past" (concerning Poe), p. 55; "lack of motivation—no concrete illustrations" (on Poe, p. 55); "story of plot and action" ("Cask of Amontillado"), p. 61; "Story of character" (Bret Harte, "Tennessee's Partner"), p. 62; "Dec. 1894 resigned from bank" (O. Henry), p. 130; "hoax plot—not in this story" (O. Henry, "Roads of Destiny"), p. 131; "phile—lover of something," p. 165; "inte-grates: character, action, & setting" (Steele), p. 179; "objec-tive" (Hemingway), p. 243; "The Education of Homer Kap-land Ross," p. 266; "episodic" (Francis), p. 267; "speed" (Rawlings), p. 283; "story of plot" (Rawlings), p. 290; "type episodic" (Johnson), p. 291; "character episodic" (on Nuhn), p. 352; "expressionistic" (Hale), p. 388; "impressionism—suggest a whole by a few broad strokes (reveals emotion character or situation with little attention to detail, with broad simplicity—with imediate subjective impressions Francophyle—lover of France" (Stevenson), pp. 422–23; "Stevenson says the short story (1) should entertain (2) [should] be convincing (3) there is no quite good book with-out morality but the world is wide & so is morality," p. 422; "title represents time limit & complication," p. 423; "Not a ballad" (Stevenson), p. 427; "master of the stream of con-sciousness" (Thomas Hardy, "Tony Kytes, the Arch-De-ceiver"), p. 441; "complications his pretty face   time—all on same road   fathers   restlessness of horse" (Hardy), p. 449; "character" (George Gissing, "The Pig and Whistle"), p. 465; "character" (Joyce), p. 483; "1943 - 1882 = 61," p. 504; "Miss Brill—Mansfield" (Stephens), p. 507; "action episo-dic   hoax plot" (Stephens), p. 509; "character" (de la Mare), p. 533; "character" (Katherine Mansfield, "Taking the Veil"), p. 573; "The Fly—Mansfield," p. 577; in "Notes and Suggestions," check marks next to "The Horses" (Steph-ens), p. 783; "A Lodging for the Night" (Stevenson), p. 780; "A Little Cloud" (Joyce), p. 782, and "The Manuscript of a Village Doctor," p. 787.

305 CERF, BENNETT A., ED. *Great Modern Short Stories: An Anthol-ogy of Twelve Famous Stories and Novelettes.* New York: Mod-ern Library 168, 1942. 480 + viii pp. W/o dj.

Signed. O'Connor has checked Henry Adams, *The Educa-tion of Henry Adams,* and Sherwood Anderson, *Winesburg, Ohio,* on catalog listing at the back of the book.

306 Ekursionen. *Ekursionen: Erzählungen unserer Zeit* (Excur-
sion: Stories of Our Time). Selected by Leonore Germann.
Munich: Carl Hanser Verlag, [1964]. 326 pp. In German.

"Everything That Rises Must Converge" is reprinted as
Überhebe ja sich keiner, pp. 283–99; biographical note, pp.
324–25.

307 Gordon, Robert, ed. *The Expanded Moment: A Short Story
Anthology.* Boston: D. C. Heath, [1963]. 310 + viii pp. Pap.

"The Artificial Nigger," pp. 256–73; questions on text,
pp. 308–9.

308 Gordon, Caroline, and Allen Tate, eds. *The House of
Fiction: An Anthology of the Short Story with Commentary by
Caroline Gordon and Allen Tate.* 2d ed. New York: Charles
Scribner's Sons, [1960] [New York, 1950]. 469 + ix pp. Pap.

Signed, dated 1960. "A Good Man Is Hard to Find," pp.
370–82; commentary "On Capote and O'Connor," pp.
382–86; biographical note, p. 467.

Letters, p. 157.

309 Lesser, M. X., and John N. Morris, eds. *Modern Short
Stories: The Fiction of Experience.* New York: McGraw-Hill,
[1962]. 460 + ix pp. Pap.

"The Artificial Nigger," pp. 128–47; comments, p. 127.

310 Lynskey, Winifred, ed. *Reading Modern Fiction: Thirty-One
Stories with Critical Aids.* 3d ed. New York: Charles Scribner's
Sons, 1962 (1952, 1957). 507 + x pp. Pap.

"A Good Man Is Hard to Find," pp. 412–25; biographical
note, p. 412; comments and questions, pp. 425–26.

311 Maugham, W. Somerset, ed. *Tellers of Tales: One Hundred
Short Stories from the United States, England, France, Russia and
Germany.* Selected, with an introduction, by Maugham.
New York: Doubleday, Doran, 1939. 1526 + xxxix pp. W/o
dj.

312 *New World Writing 19.* Ed. Stewart Richardson and Corlies
M. Smith. Philadelphia: J. B. Lippincott, Keystone KB33,
[1961]. 219 pp. Pap.

"Everything That Rises Must Converge," pp. 74–90; biographical note, p. 74.

Letters, pp. 436, 438, 453, 462, 555, 575, 589.

313 *New World Writing*. Ed. Arabel J. Porter. New York: New American Library, Mentor Ms73, 1952. 315 + viii pp. Pap. Illus.

Includes "Enoch and the Gorilla" from *Wise Blood*, pp. 67–74; biographical note, p. 67.

Letters, pp. 31, 33.

314 ———. Copy 2.

315 *New World Writing*. Ed. Arabel J. Porter. New York: New American Library, Mentor MD146, [1955]. 218 pp. Pap.

Signed on front cover "Regina O'Connor." Includes "You Can't Be Any Poorer Than Dead," first version of opening chapter of *The Violent Bear It Away*, pp. 81–97; biographical note, p. 81.

Letters, pp. 77, 79, 81, 104, 142, 367, 589.

316 ———. Copy 2.

Lines crossed out in O'Connor's story: "dwarf" (line 20, p. 87); "and each . . . steak" (lines 30–31, p. 90); "What . . . piece?" (lines 1–2, p. 92).

317 RAHV, PHILIP, ED. *Eight Great American Short Novels*. Introduction by Rahv. New York: Berkley Publishing, Medallion N742, 1963. 414 pp. Pap.

Wise Blood, pp. 244–358; comments on O'Connor by Rahv, pp. 15–16; biographical note, p. 414.

Letters, p. 522.

318 ———. Copy 2.

319 O'BRIEN, CONOR CRUISE. *Maria Cross: Imaginative Patterns in a Group of Modern Catholic Writers*. Fresno, Calif.: Academy Guild Press, 1963 (London, 1954). 259 + xi pp. Pap.

Underlining, p. 87.

320 CRANE, R. S., W. R. KEAST, RICHARD McKEON, NORMAN MacLEAN, ELDER OLSON, AND BERNARD WEINBERG. *Critics*

and Criticism: Essays in Method. Abridged edition. Chicago: University of Chicago Press, Phoenix P15, 1960 (1952, 1957). 276 + vii pp. Pap.

Marginal lining, p. 19. Check marks, p. 19.

"The first results whenever we want to know either the event or the circumstances of the event, whether in past, present, or future time; hence the poet must avoid the necessary, the impossible, or the completely probable, or that which is unimportant either way, for we are never in suspense about these; instead, he must choose the equally probable or else that which is probable with a chance of its not happening, and something which is of a markedly pleasant, painful, good, evil, or marvelous nature. Suspense of the second order is produced by unexpected frustration, by having the thing seem just about to happen, and then probably averting it. The anticipated thing must have importance exceeding the suspense; otherwise irritation and indifference result" (marginal lining, p. 19; in Elder Olson, "An Outline of Poetic Theory").

321 KAZIN, ALFRED. *The Inmost Leaf: A Selection of Essays.* New York: Harcourt, Brace, 1955. 273 + viii pp.

Signed "F. O'Connor, Milledgeville."

322 PRAZ, MARIO. *The Flaming Heart: Essays on Crashaw, Machiavelli, and Other Studies in the Relations between Italian and English Literature from Chaucer to T. S. Eliot.* Garden City, N.Y.: Doubleday, Anchor A132, 1958. 390 pp. Pap.

323 TATE, ALLEN. *The Forlorn Demon: Didactic and Critical Essays.* Chicago: Henry Regnery, 1953. 180 + vii pp.

Signed, dated 1953.

324 WILSON, EDMUND. *Axel's Castle: A Study in the Imaginative Literature of 1870–1930.* New York: Charles Scribner's Sons, 1947 [New York, 1931]. 319 pp. W/o dj.

Index pages uncut.

Signed, dated September 1947.

325 Blackmur, R. P. *Anni Mirabiles, 1921–1925: Reason in the Madness of Letters.* Washington: Library of Congress, 1956. 55 pp. Pap. Pamphlet.

Four lectures sponsored by the Gertrude Clarke Whittall Poetry and Literature Fund.

326 Richards, I. A. *Practical Criticism: A Study of Literary Judgment.* New York: Harcourt, Brace and World, Harvest HB16, n.d. (1929). 362 + xiv pp. Pap.

327 Santayana, George. *Three Philosophical Poets: Lucretius, Dante, and Goethe.* Cambridge: Harvard University Press, 1945 [1910]. 215 + viii pp.

Signed, dated 1946. Marking on back inside cover: "1OPEN6." Marginal lining, p. 153. Underlining, p. 157. Marginalia: "Poe," p. 12; "Poe refuted," p. 12; "rather it would never have been expressed," p. 143; "not Faust," p. 145; "naïeve of brother Santayana," p. 153; "end result: Dr. Mathew Mighty-grain-of-salt Dante O'Connor;—Teresius," p. 156.

"Any great scope he can attain must be due to his powers of representation. His understanding may render him universal; his life never can" (underlining, p. 157; concerning Faust).

328 Jarrell, Randall. *Poetry and the Age.* New York: Vintage K-12, 1955 (New York, 1953). 246 + viii pp. Pap.

329 Fergusson, Francis. *The Idea of a Theater, A Study of Ten Plays: The Art of Drama in Changing Perspective.* Garden City, N.Y.: Doubleday, Anchor A4, 1953 [Princeton, 1949]. 255 pp. Pap.

330 Brooks, Cleanth, and Robert Penn Warren. *Understanding Fiction.* 2d ed. New York: Appleton-Century-Crofts, 1959. 688 + xxiii pp. W/o dj.

Signed, dated 1960. Includes "A Good Man Is Hard to Find," pp. 355–67; interpretation and questions, pp. 367–68. *Letters,* pp. 83, 192, 283.

331 Lubbock, Percy. *The Craft of Fiction.* New York: Peter Smith, 1945 [1921]. [277] pp. W/o dj.

Signed, dated 1947. Marginal linings on pp. 18, 19, 20, 21, 38, 39, 40, 41, 44, 48, 53–54, 62–63, 63–64, 64–67, 68, 69, 71–72, 72, 73, 74, 75, 80, 81, 82, 83, 84, 85, 86, 87–89, 90, 91, 92, 99, 100, 101, 102, 103, 104, 111, 112, 113, 115, 147. Check marks, pp. 7, 9, 10, 11, 12, 14, 15, 16, 17, 18, 23, 27, 31, 38, 140, 252.

"And upon these trophies he sets to work with the full force of his imagination; he detects their significance, he disengages and throws aside whatever is accidental and meaningless; he re-makes them in conditions that are never known in life, conditions in which a thing is free to grow according to its own law, expressing itself unhindered; he liberates and completes. And then, upon all this new life— so like the old and yet so different, *more* like the old, as one may say, than the old ever had the chance of being—upon all this life that is now so much more intensely living than before, Tolstoy directs the skill of his art" (marginal lining, p. 18).

"The whole point of the action is in its representative character, its universality; this it must plainly wear" (marginal lining, p. 44).

"Two people, an elderly man of the world and a scheming hostess, are talking together, the room fills, a young man enters; or in another sociable assembly there is a shriek and a rush, and the children of the house charge into the circle; that is quite enough for Tolstoy, his drama of youth and age opens immediately with the right impression. The story is in movement without delay; there are a few glimpses of this kind, and then the scene is ready, the action may go forward; everything is attuned for the effect it is to make.

"And at the other end of the book, after many hundreds of pages, the story is brought to a full close in an episode which gathers up all the threads and winds them together. The youths and maidens are now the parents of another riotous brood. Not one of them has ended where he or she expected to end, but their lives have taken a certain shape, and it is unmistakable that this shape is final. Nothing more will happen to them which an onlooker cannot easily foretell" (marginal lining, pp. 53–54; concerning *War and Peace*).

"I speak of his 'telling' the story, but of course he has no idea of doing that and no more; the art of fiction does not begin until the novelist thinks of his story as a matter to be *shown*, to be so exhibited that it will tell itself. To hand over to the reader the facts of the story merely as so much information—this is no more than to state the 'argument' of the book, the groundwork upon which the novelist proceeds to create. The book is not a row of facts, it is a single image; the facts have no validity in themselves, they are nothing until they have been used. It is not the simple art of narrative, but the comprehensive art of fiction that I am considering; and in fiction there can be no appeal to any authority outside the book itself. Narrative—like the tales of Defoe, for example—must look elsewhere for support; Defoe produced it by the assertion of the historic truthfulness of his stories. But in a novel, strictly so called, attestation of this kind is, of course, quite irrelevant; the thing has to *look* true, and that is all. It is not made to look true by simple statement" (marginal lining, p. 62).

"The matter would then be objective and visible to the reader, instead of reaching him in the form of a report at second hand. But how to manage this without falling back upon the author and *his* report, which has already been tried and for good reasons, as it seemed, abandoned? It is managed by a kind of repetition of the same stroke, a further shift of the point of view. The spectator, the listener, the reader, is now himself to be placed at the angle of vision; not an account or a report, more or less convincing, is to be offered him, but a direct sight of the matter itself, while it is passing" (passage noted by check mark, p. 252). *Letters*, p. 192.

332 BEACH, JOSEPH WARREN. *The Twentieth Century Novel: Studies in Technique*. New York: D. Appleton-Century, [1933]. 569 + viii pp. W/o dj.

Signed. Marginal lining, p. 98. Underlinings, pp. 4, 6, 20, 26, 409, 447.

"James, in 'The Ambassadors,' turns pictorial matter into drama by straining it through the consciousness of the leading character" (underlining, p. 6).

"One feature only I will mention, and that is the character of Svidrigaïlov. It illustrates so well Dostoevski's unfailing instinct, whenever he has an abstract principle to develop, for inventing a real character to be its embodiment. Raskolnikov, his leading character, he wishes to be on the whole sympathetic to the reader. His very sensitiveness of nature makes him all the more liable to an unfaith which is the measure of his sympathy for miserable humanity. The same thing is true of Ivan Karamazov. But in both cases Dostoevski wishes us to understand the profound moral ugliness implied in the man's religious position; he wishes man to understand it himself. And in each case he has used the same device for shadowing forth this necessary truth. For each of these men he has provided a kind of obscene double or shadow. For Ivan Karamazov it is Smerdyakov; for Raskolnikov it is Svidrigaïlov" (marginal lining, p. 98).

333 FORSTER, E. M. *Aspects of the Novel*. New York: Harcourt, Brace, Harvest HB 19, [1954] [New York, 1927]. 176 pp. Pap.

334 JAMES, HENRY. *The Future of the Novel: Essays on the Art of Fiction*. Ed., with an introduction, by Leon Edel. New York: Vintage K41, 1956. [287] + xviii + v pp. Pap.

Marginal linings on pp. 193, 195, 196–97, 198, 202, 203, 204, 205, 207, 212, 240, 249. Underlinings on pp. 193, 195, 240.

"In fine, his readers must be grateful to him for such a passage as that in which he remarks that whereas the public at large very legitimately says to a writer, 'Console me, amuse me, terrify me, make me cry, make me dream, or make me think,' what the sincere critic says is, 'Make me something fine in the form that shall suit you best, according to your temperament.' This seems to me to put into a nutshell the whole question of the different classes of fiction, concerning which there has recently been so much discourse. There are simply as many different kinds as there are persons practicing the art, for if a picture, a tale, or a novel be a direct impression of life (and that surely constitutes its interest and value), the impression will vary according to the plate that takes it, the particular structure and mixture of the recipient" (marginal lining, also partly underlined, p. 195).

"Every good story is of course both a picture and an idea, and the more they are interfused the better the problem is solved" (circled, p. 212).

Letters, pp. 103, 157, 236.

335 PARIS REVIEW. *Writers at Work: The "Paris Review" Interviews.* Ed., with an introduction, by Malcolm Cowley. New York: Viking Press, 1958. 309 pp.

Letters, p. 293.

336 BABBITT, IRVING. *Rousseau and Romanticism.* New York: Meridian M3, 1955 (1919). 324 pp. Pap.

Marginal linings on pp. 259, 265. Underlinings on pp. 154, 262.

" 'I wish to see man as he is,' she [George Sand] writes to Flaubert. 'He is not good or bad: he is good and bad. But he is something else besides: being good and bad he has an inner force which leads him to be very bad and a little good, or very good and a little bad. I have often wondered,' she adds, 'why your "Education Sentimentale" was so ill received by the public, and the reason, as it seems to me, is that its characters are passive—that they do not act upon themselves' " (marginal lining, p. 259).

337 PRAZ, MARIO. *The Romantic Agony*. Trans. Angus Davidson. New York: Meridian MG5, 1956 (1933). 502 + xix pp. Pap.
Marginal lining on p. 121.
Letters, p. 229.

338 DILLISTONE, F. W. *The Novelist and the Passion Story: A Study of Christ Figures in Faulkner, Mauriac, Melville, and Kazantzakis*. New York: Sheed and Ward, [1960]. 128 pp.
Signed, "F. O'Connor 1961."
Bulletin, 12.23.61, p. 6; *Reviews*, pp. 127–28.

339 JARRET-KERR, MARTIN, C. R. *Studies in Literature and Belief*. London: Rockliff, [1954]. 203 + xi pp.
Signed "F. O'Connor 1959." Marginal linings on pp. 172, 175, 177. Check mark on p. 173.
"What I have called the erosion of the imaginative soil has affected the self-consciously Catholic writers we have been considering in a further sense; they are incapable of full-blooded doubt. What, in fact, one is most conscious of in them is a deficiency of that creative scepticism which was described by Donne (leaning on St. Augustine): 'Would you know of a truth? Doubt, and then you will inquire. . . . As no man resolves of any thing wisely, firmly, safely, of which he never doubted, never debated, so neither doth God withdraw a resolution from any man, that doubts with an humble purpose to settle his own faith, and not with a wrangling purpose to shake another man's' " (marginal lining, p. 172).
Letters, p. 297.

340 *Studi Americani*, vol. 2. Rome: Edizioni di Storia e Letteratura, 1956. 301 pp. Pap. In Italian.
Most pages uncut.

341 ENGLE, PAUL, ED. *Midland: Twenty-Five Years of Fiction and Poetry Selected from the Writing Workshops of the State University of Iowa*. Assisted by Henri Coulette and Donald Justice. New York: Random House, 1961. 600 + xxxvii pp.

Signed, dated 1961. Includes "The Artificial Nigger," pp. 209–32; and contributor's note: "Flannery O'Connor has published her work virtually everywhere, in most distinguished magazines. She lives in Georgia and raises fowl," p. 593.

342 SUMMERS, HOLLIS, AND EDGAR WHAN, EDS. *Literature: An Introduction.* New York: McGraw-Hill, 1960. 706 + xx pp. W/o dj.

Checked in table of contents: Eudora Welty, "A Visit of Charity"; Flannery O'Connor, "The River" (pp. 30–39); Katherine Anne Porter, "That Tree"; Jessamyn West, "Love, Death, and the Ladies' Drill Team" (with marginal note, "credit?"); Peter Taylor, "The Unforgivable"; T. S. Eliot, "Animula" and "Journey of the Magi"; E. E. Cummings, "love is more thicker than forget"; Richard Wilbur, "Clearness" and "The Pardon"; Robert Lowell, "Mr. Edwards and the Spider."

343 TATE, ALLEN, ED. *A Southern Vanguard.* John Peale Bishop Memorial Volume. New York: Prentice-Hall, [1947]. 331 + [xi] pp.

Signed. Underlinings, pp. 109, 110. Marginal notations, pp. 105, 114.

"Formality becomes a condition of survival" (circled in McLuhan, p. 110).

Letters, pp. 70, 174.

344 NEW SIGNATURES. SWALLOW, ALAN, ED. *New Signatures 1948: A Selection of College Writing.* Vol. 1. Prairie City, Ill.: Press of James A. Decker [1948]. 178 + xiii pp. W/o dj.

Signed. Includes "The Barber," pp. 113–24.

345 BRODIN, PIERRE. *Présences contemporaines: Écrivains Américains d'Aujourd'hui (Contemporary Presences: American Writers Today).* Paris: Les Nouvelles Éditions Debresse, 1964. 219 pp. Pap. Photographs. In French.

Essay on O'Connor, pp. 123–33; letter (in English) from

O'Connor on French influences in her writing, pp. 206–7; listing of criticism on O'Connor in French, pp. 217–18.

"I think that the character of Old Tarwater in *The Violent Bear It Away* owes something to Léon Bloy, however far removed I may be from him in regard to culture" (p. 207).

346 FOERSTER, NORMAN. *Image of America: Our Literature from Puritanism to the Space Age.* Notre Dame, Ind.: University of Notre Dame Press, Notre Dame Paperback 16, 1962 (1934). 152 + v pp. Pap.

Marginal linings, pp. 50, 57, 69–70, 81, 87, 104. Check mark, p. 71.

Bulletin, 9.26.63, pp. 162–63.

347 GARDINER, HAROLD C., S.J., ED. *American Classics Reconsidered: A Christian Appraisal.* New York: Charles Scribner's Sons, 1958. 307 + x pp.

Signed. Marginal lining, p. 3. Brackets, p. 3. Article on Thoreau titled "*Christian* Malgré Lui," by Michael F. Moloney, pp. 193–209.

Bulletin, 11.1.58; *Reviews*, pp. 59–60.

348 LAWRENCE, D. H. *Studies in Classic American Literature.* Garden City, N.Y.: Doubleday, Anchor A5, 1953 [New York, 1923]. 191 pp.

349 WINTERS, YVOR. *In Defense of Reason.* Denver: University of Denver Press, Swallow Press, 1947 [1937]. 611 + viii pp.

Signed, dated 1958. Includes *Primitivism and Decadence; Maule's Curse; The Anatomy of Nonsense; The Significance of "The Bridge."*

Letters, pp. 286–87.

350 BROOKS, CLEANTH. *The Hidden God: Studies in Hemingway, Faulkner, Yeats, Eliot, and Warren.* New Haven: Yale University Press, Yale Paperbound Y-87, 1963. 136 + xi pp. Pap.

"F. O'Connor 947 City" written on label which reads "Employ Epileptics" and is pasted to outside front cover.

351 RUBIN, LOUIS D., JR., AND ROBERT D. JACOBS, EDS. *South:*

Modern Southern Literature in Its Cultural Setting. Garden City, N.Y.: Doubleday, Dolphin C316, 1961. 440 pp. Pap.

Discussion of O'Connor by Walter Sullivan, pp. 379–80; selected bibliography of O'Connor's works and work on her, p. 417.

352 RYAN, ABRAM J. *Poems: Patriotic, Religious, Miscellaneous.* New York: P. J. Kenedy and Sons, [1896] [1880]. 360 + xxxviii pp. Illus. W/o dj.

Memoir of Father Ryan by John Moran.

353 ELIOT, T. S. *Collected Poems, 1909–1935.* New York: Harcourt, Brace, [1936]. 220 pp. W/o dj.

Signed. Possibly used as a college text. Underlining, p. 43. Marginalia: "Measure for Measure Act III" (for epigraph, "Gerontion"), p. 43; "Little old man," p. 43; "free-thinking Jew," p. 43; "WRATH," p. 43; "commercial" (in "The Fire Sermon," lines 211–12), p. 79; "Eng. children say this on Guy Fawks day and carry an effigy of G.F.—similar to Halloween antics" (to "The Hollow Men"), p. 101; "*Essays*—Yeats *Theosophical System*—Yeats *Yeats Autobiographies*" (back endpaper); "highly technical discipline," inside back cover.

354 ———. *The Cultivation of Christmas Trees.* New York: Farrar, Straus and Cudahy, [1956]. [7] pp. W/o dj.

Typography, binding, and decorations by Enrico Arno. Marked "First Edition."

355 ———. *Four Quartets.* New York: Harcourt, Brace, [1943]. 39 pp.

Signed.

356 ———. *The Waste Land and Other Poems.* New York: Harcourt, Brace, Harvest HB1, [1934]. 88 pp.

357 FITZGERALD, ROBERT. *In the Rose of Time: Poems, 1931–1956.* Norfolk, Conn.: James Laughlin, New Directions, [1956]. 150 pp.

"To Flannery O'Connor In memory of the redemption of Hazel Motes   Robert Fitzgerald" on flyleaf.

358 LOWELL, ROBERT. *Life Studies*. New York: Farrar, Straus and Cudahy, 1959. 90 pp. Water damaged.

Letters, pp. 321, 335–36.

359 ———. *Lord Weary's Castle*. 2d ed. New York: Harcourt, Brace, 1946. 69 + ix pp. Water damaged.

Signed, dated 1949.

360 ———. *The Mills of the Kavanaughs*. New York: Harcourt, Brace, 1951. 55 pp.

Signed.

Letters, pp. 26, 152.

361 MEREDITH, WILLIAM. *The Open Sea and Other Poems*. New York: Alfred A. Knopf, 1958. 60 + vii pp.

362 BELLAMANN, KATHERINE. *A Poet Passed This Way*. Mill Valley, Calif.: Wings Press, 1958. 134 pp.

"Henry H. Bellamann Special Award Presented to—Flannery O'Connor to recognize and encourage unusual artistic talent   April 1964" written in formal hand on flyleaf.

363 PERCY, WILLIAM ALEXANDER. *Sappho in Levkas and Other Poems*. New Haven: Yale University Press, 1925 (1915). 78 + x pp.

364 STEVENS, WALLACE. BROWN, ASHLEY, AND ROBERT S. HALLER, EDS. *The Achievement of Wallace Stevens*. Philadelphia: J. B. Lippincott, 1962. 287 pp.

365 BOCK, FREDERICK. *The Fountains of Regardlessness*. New York: Macmillan Poets MP64, 1961. 70 + viii pp. Pap.

366 MAURA, SISTER M., S.S.N.D. *The Word Is Love*. New York: Macmillan, 1958. 52 + viii pp.

"For Flannery O'Connor, who knows by what mysterious ways God speaks His word. Sister Maura." on flyleaf.

367 MONTGOMERY, MARION. *Dry Lightning*. First-Book Poetry Series, vol 2. Lincoln: University of Nebraska Press, 1960. 80 + viii pp. Pap.

"For Flannery O'Connor, with admiration and best regards. Marion Montgomery, December 5, 1960" on title page.

368 O'GORMAN, NED. *The Night of the Hammer*. New York: Harcourt, Brace, [1959]. 44 pp.

The Lamont Poetry Selection for 1958.

Letters, p. 355.

369 TABOR, EITHNE. *The Cliff's Edge: Songs of a Psychotic*. New York: Sheed and Ward, 1959 [New York, 1950]. 80 pp. Pap.

Front cover and title page signed "Janet McKa[ne]." Marginalia: "Mary-Schizophrenia   Others   Alter Christus" listed on back endpaper.

Letters, p. 512.

370 ELIOT, T. S. *The Confidential Clerk*. New York: Harcourt, Brace, [1954]. 159 pp.

Signed, dated April 1954.

371 ———. *The Elder Statesman*. New York: Farrar, Straus and Cudahy, 1959. 134 pp.

Enclosed: a slip reading "With the compliments of Robert Giroux."

372 ———. *Murder in the Cathedral*. 2d ed., rev. New York: Harcourt, Brace, [1936]. 86 pp.

Signed, dated 1950.

Letters, p. 23.

373 ELIOT, T. S., AND GEORGE HOELLERING. *The Film of Murder in the Cathedral*. Preface by Eliot. Preface by Hoellering. New York: Harcourt, Brace, [1952] [New York, 1936]. 110 + xv + [48] pp. Illus.

Signed, dated 1952.

374 BEST. FOLEY, MARTHA, AND DAVID BURNETT, EDS. *The Best American Short Stories 1962 and the Yearbook of the American Short Story*. New York: Ballantine, Dolphin S695, 1962. 414 + viii pp. Pap.

Includes "Everything That Rises Must Converge," pp. 308–21; biographical note, p. 397.

375 DWADZIEŚCIA SZEŚĆ. 26: *wspótczesnych opowiadań amerykań-skich* (*Twenty-six: Modern American Stories*), ed. Maxim Lieber. Warsaw: Iskry, 1963. [577] pp. Pap. In Polish.

Includes "Poczciwi wieśniacy" ("Good Country People"), pp. 552–77; biographical note, p. [551].

376 SOME. MEDLEY, STANLEY, ED. *Some Postwar American Writers.* Stockholm: Sveriges Radio, 1962. 168 pp. Pap. In English.

Includes "Good Country People" in excerpted form, pp. 13–19; portrait of O'Connor, p. 10; biographical introduction, pp. 11–13.

377 ———. Copy 2.

378 CASSILL, R. V., HERBERT GOLD, AND JAMES B. HALL. *Fifteen by Three.* New York: James Laughlin, New Directions 68, [1957]. 248 + viii pp. Pap.

379 GOLD, HERBERT, ED. *Fiction of the Fifties: A Decade of American Writing.* Introduction by Gold. Garden City, N.Y.: Doubleday, Dolphin C299, 1961. 392 pp. Pap.

Written on front cover: "p. 287." Includes "The Artificial Nigger," pp. 287–309; O'Connor's note to the reader, p. 27; biographical note, p. 287.

380 WEST, RAY B., JR., ED. *American Short Stories.* Introduction by West. New York: Thomas Y. Crowell, [1959]. 267 + viii pp.

Includes "The Life You Save May Be Your Own," pp. 259–65; biographical note, p. 258.

381 CHASE, RICHARD. *The American Novel and Its Tradition.* Garden City, N.Y.: Doubleday, Anchor A116, [1957]. 266 + xii pp. Pap.

Marginal linings on pp. x, xi, 8. Arrows on pp. 25n, 27, 41, 82.

"These qualities have made romance a suitable, even, as it seems, an inevitable, vehicle for the intellectual and moral ideas of the American novelists. They have used romance to introduce into the novel what one may roughly describe as the narrow profundity of New England Puritanism, the skeptical, rationalistic spirit of the Enlightenment, and the imaginative freedom of Transcendentalism. In doing so they have created a brilliant and original, if often unstable and fragmentary, kind of literature" (marginal lining, p. x).

"It is not necessarily true that in so far as a novel departs from realism it is obscurantist and disqualified to make moral comments on the world" (marginal lining, p. xi).

"Cf. Melville's plea to his reality-minded readers for latitude in the depiction of character and incident. The ideal reader, he says, will 'want nature . . . ; but nature unfettered, exhilarated, in effect transformed. . . . It is with fiction as with religion, it should present another world, and yet one to which we feel the tie.' (*The Confidence Man* [by Melville], Chapter 33.)" (arrow, p. 25n).

"The great novelist responds to the 'need of performing his whole possible revolution, by the law of some rich passion in him for extremes' " (arrow, p. 27, quoting Henry James).

Letters, pp. 408, 411.

382 HUBBELL, JAY B. *Southern Life in Fiction.* Athens: University of Georgia Press, 1960. 99 + xii pp.

Eugenia Dorothy Blount Lamar Memorial Lectures, 1959; delivered at Mercer University on November 17, 18, and 19. Lecture 3 on "Georgia in Literature."

Signed "F. O'Connor, 1960."

383 TURNER, ARLIN, ED. *Southern Stories.* Introduction by Turner. New York: Rinehart 106, [1960]. 336 + xl pp. Pap.

Includes "Greenleaf," pp. 313–36; biographical note, p. 313.

Letters, pp. 546, 589.

384 WARREN, ROBERT PENN, AND ALBERT ERSKINE, EDS. *A New Southern Harvest.* New York: Bantam F1556, [1957]. 294 + ix pp. Pap.

Includes "The Life You Save May Be Your Own," pp. 249–58; biographical note, p. 293.

385 LEVIN, HARRY. *The Power of Blackness: Hawthorne, Poe, Melville*. New York: Vintage K-90, 1960 (New York, 1958). 263 + xii + ix pp. Pap.

Marginal linings on pp. 7, 8, 17, 27, 78. Marginalia: "devil doing the work for grace before," p. 78.

"If the minister cannot shrive himself, the physician has a disease he cannot cure. Yet it is his concentrated malevolence, more than anything else, that implants the idea of confessing in Dimmesdale's mind. Whether Chillingworth may be his double or else a demon, the spokesman for Dimmesdale's conscience or a devil's emissary—these are possibilities which are raised but scarcely probed. He himself concedes that he is performing a fiend-like office, but considers this 'a dark necessity,' the inevitable consequence of Hester's downfall, perhaps of Calvinistic predestination" (marginal lining, with annotation, p. 78).

386 HAWTHORNE, NATHANIEL. JAMES, HENRY. *Hawthorne*. Garden City, N.Y.: Doubleday, Dolphin C58, [n.d.]. 154 pp. Pap.

Marginal linings on pp. 57, 58, 102. Underlining on p. 57. Check marks on pp. 10, 16, 18. Marginalia: "Poe," p. 58.

"This moral is that the flower of art blooms only where the soil is deep, that it takes a great deal of history to produce a little literature, that it needs a complex social machinery to set a writer in motion" (check mark, p. 10).

"To him as to them, the consciousness of *sin* was the most importunate fact of life" (check mark, p. 16).

"Hawthorne, in his metaphysical moods, is nothing if not allegorical, and allegory, to my sense, is quite one of the lighter exercises of the imagination" (marginal lining, also partly underlined, p. 57).

". . . in such a process discretion is everything, and when the image becomes importunate it is in danger of seeming to stand for nothing more serious than itself" (marginal lining, p. 102).

387 ———. Van Doren, Mark. *Nathaniel Hawthorne.* New York: Viking Press, Compass C23, 1957 [New York, 1949]. 279 + [viii] pp. Pap.

Signed, dated 1963. Marginal linings on pp. 62, 63, 67, 126, 128, 148, 172, 178, 179. Check marks on pp. 66, 127.

"Hawthorne had cultivated in himself a weakness for the abstract. Abstraction is necessary to narrative, but at a deeper level than any which the poet lets us see. It is what makes the people finally important and utterly exciting. But exhibited before our eyes, in the refractory medium of accident and character, of speech and deed, it distracts us so that we can neither believe nor feel. In *The Scarlet Letter* Hawthorne has at last found individuals who can hold all of his thought, and so naturally that even he forgets what his thought is. His thought can be of them, not what they signify" (marginal lining, p. 148).

"By usable truth, we mean the apprehension of the absolute condition of present things as they strike the eye of the man who fears them not, though they do their worst to him. . . . There is the grand truth about Nathaniel Hawthorne. He says no! in thunder; but the Devil himself cannot make him say yes. For all men who say *yes,* lie" (marginal lining, p. 178, quoting Melville).

"Behind those eyes, said Melville, there was 'a blackness ten-times black,' a 'great power of blackness' that derived from Hawthorne's peculiar 'calvinistic sense of Innate Depravity and Original Sin, from whose visitations, in some shape or other, no deeply thinking mind is always and wholly free. . . . Perhaps no writer has ever wielded this terrific thought with greater terror than this same harmless Hawthorne' " (marginal lining, quoting Melville, p. 179).

388 James, Henry. *The Notebooks of Henry James.* Ed., with an introduction, by F. O. Matthiessen and Kenneth B. Murdock. New York: George Braziller, 1955 (New York, 1947). 425 + xxviii pp. W/o dj.

"Margaret Lee (?)" on flyleaf. Marginal linings on pp. xi, xii, xvii, xviii, 48, 102, 106. Underlinings on pp. xi, xvii, 101. Marginalia: "X!" p. xi; "Note!" p. xii; exclamation mark, pp. 101, 102, 106; "people?" p. 422. Checked in index: pp. xv, 46–49 (to *The Bostonians*), p. 421; Guy Domville, Hawthorne, James Russell Lowell, John Delavoy (with "people?" in margin), *The Jolly Corner, Notes of a Son and Brother, On the Death of Dumas the Younger, Owen Wingrave, The Princess Casamassima, The Sacred Fount, The Spoils of Poynton,* p. 422; *The Turn of the Screw, The Wings of the Dove,* p. 423.

"He knew that the fruitful generalization can be reached only through an abundant sequence of details, that the theoretical must be drenched with the actual" (marginal lining, annotated, p. xii).

"He often invoked 'the spirit of Maupassant' to come to his aid, and though his desire to portray a more and more intricate consciousness inevitably led him into greater length, he kept from first to last, to his resolution to be 'intensely objective' " (marginal lining, also partly underlined, p. xvii).

"She was heroic, she was sublime, the whole moral history of Boston was reflected in her displaced spectacles" (marginal lining, quoting *The Bostonians,* p. 48).

"Action which is never dialogue and dialogue which is always action" (marginal lining, with exclamation point, p. 102).

389 ———. WARD, J. A. *The Imagination of Disaster: Evil in the Fiction of Henry James.* Lincoln: University of Nebraska Press, 1962 (1961). 185 + xi pp.

"Nov. 21, 1962. For Flannery O'Connor, with admiration and gratitude (and some misgivings about putting this book in your hands). Jack Ward" on flyleaf.

390 HICKS, GRANVILLE, ED. *The Living Novel: A Symposium.* Foreword by Hicks. New York: Macmillan, 1957. 230 + xii pp.

Bottom half of pp. 225–26 missing.

Signed "F. O'Connor." Marginal lining on p. 162; underlining, p. 162. Includes "The Fiction Writer and His Country," pp. 157–64; biographical note, p. 229.

    Letters, pp. 201–2, 205–6, 251, 253, 256, 270.

391 DORRANCE, WARD, AND THOMAS MABRY. *The White Hound.*
Introduction by Caroline Gordon. Columbia: University of
Missouri Press, 1959. 205 + xiv pp.

    Comment on O'Connor, p. xiii.

392 PRIZE STORIES. POIRIER, RICHARD, ED. *Prize Stories, 1963: The
O. Henry Awards.* Introduction by Poirier. Garden City,
N.Y.: Doubleday, 1963. 263 + xvi pp.

    Includes "Everything That Rises Must Converge" as first
prize winner, pp. [1]–16; biographical note, p. [1].

    Letters, pp. 510, 511.

393 FULLER, EDMUND. *Man in Modern Fiction: Some Minority
Opinions on Contemporary American Writing.* New York: Ran-
dom House, Vintage V177, [1958], [1949], 171 + xvii pp.
Pap.

    Marginal lining, p. 10. Brackets, pp. 9–10, 14. Check
marks, pp. 7, 9, 14.

    "The writer cannot be wholly coherent, as artist, unless
he possesses a wholly coherent view of man to inform,
illuminate, and integrate his work" (check mark, p. 7).

394 PRESCOTT, ORVILLE, ED. *Mid-Century: An Anthology of Distinguished Contemporary American Short Stories.* New York:
Pocket Library PL65, 1958. 320 + xi pp. Pap.

    Signed on front cover. Includes "The River," pp. 90–107;
critical commentary, p. 90.

395 BRAGDON, CLAUDE. *Merely Players.* New York: Alfred A.
Knopf, 1929. 215 + xv pp. Illus. W/o dj.

    Label for "Miller's Book Store Atlanta Ga." on inside
front cover.

396 JAMES, HENRY. *The Letters of Henry James.* Ed. Percy Lubbock, Vol. 2. New York: Charles Scribner's Sons, 1920. 511
+ xi pp. W/o dj.

Crossed out on flyleaf: "Minnie Bullock May H. Yar-
borough Becky Harnoy [?]." Written on flyleaf: "Lucy
Gragg Ida Munro." *The book is heavily marked, but markings
may not be O'Connor's,* although she would have noticed
them. Marginal linings on pp. 9, 10, 11, 15, 17, 20, 26, 27,
31, 36, 39, 43, 45, 46, 48, 57, 62, 63, 65, 66, 68, 69, 70, 71, 73,
81, 83, 85, 86, 91, 93, 94, 95, 96, 99, 100, 101, 104, 106, 108,
112, 113, 115, 116, 117, 118, 119, 120, 124, 125, 126, 127, 128,
129, 130, 131, 136, 137, 138, 139–40, 140, 141, 142, 143, 147,
159, 160, 167, 175, 180, 181, 198, 202, 203, 207, 209, 210, 224,
225, 226, 227, 228, 230, 233, 237, 238, 240, 242, 243, 244, 245,
249, 251, 253, 256, 258, 259, 263, 266, 268, 270, 273, 276, 281,
282, 283, 284, 289, 291, 294, 299, 301, 306, 308, 318, 320, 323,
324, 327, 333, 334, 335, 336, 337, 338, 342, 343, 344, 353, 354,
355, 359, 362, 372, 373, 375, 376, 377, 382, 384, 385, 386, 387,
388, 389, 390, 391, 393, 399, 401, 402, 403, 406, 408, 409, 411,
415, 416, 417, 418, 419, 420, 421, 423, 424, 426, 427, 428, 429,
430, 438, 439, 441, 442, 443, 445, 446, 447, 448, 451, 455, 462,
463, 471, 472, 473, 476, 478, 480, 481, 482, 484, 485, 486, 488,
489, 490, 492, 495, 497, 498, 499. Underlinings on pp. 124,
141, 181, 224, 275, 283, 335, 342, 351, 361, 473, 511. Check
marks on pp. 9, 11, 15, 20, 23, 35, 75, 77, 80, 83, 91, 117, 119,
121, 123, 141, 147, 250, 285, 342, 403, 408, 503, 504, 517.
Marginalia (not in O'Connor's hand): "Aunt Ann 1892," p.
234; "see Vol I pp–138," p. 275; "compare with *Real Right
Thing,*" p. 346; "1903," p. 503; "1876," p. 503; "Process a
real operation [erasure] would hope come out all right Love
L.," p. 510; "195 American understanding 240 Golden
Bowl Wings of the Dove 277 American Scene Criticism
of style 299 enthusiasm over American Scene Life &
works Relations to Contemporaries Course of his development," back end paper. Many check marks in index not
in O'Connor's hand.

"I am hungry for Material, whatever I may be moved to
do with it; and, honestly, I think, there will not be an inch

or an ounce of it unlikely to prove grist to my intellectual and 'artistic' mill" (marginal linings, p. 9).

"I adore a rounded objectivity, a completely and patiently achieved one" (marginal lining and partly underlined, p. 334).

"Of course for myself I live, live intensely and am fed by life, and my value, whatever it be, is in my own kind of expression of that" (marginal lining, p. 489).

Letters, pp. 103, 383.

397 STEGNER, WALLACE, ED. *Selected American Prose, 1841–1900: The Realistic Movement*. Introduction by Stegner. New York: Rinehart 94, [1958]. 343 + xxviii pp. Pap.

398 DONNE, JOHN. *The Complete Poetry and Selected Prose of John Donne*. Ed., with an introduction, by Charles M. Coffin. New York: Modern Library 12, [1952]. 594 + xliii pp.

Marginal lining, p. 153.

"How happy'is hee, which hath due placed assign'd / To'his beasts, and disaforested his minde!" (bracketed, p. 153).

399 CHESTERTON. KENNER, HUGH. *Paradox in Chesterton*. Introduction by Herbert Marshall McLuhan. London: Sheed and Ward, 1948. 156 + xxii pp.

400 TINDALL, WILLIAM YORK. *Forces in Modern British Literature: 1885–1956*. New York: Vintage K35, 1956. 316 + vii + xx pp. Pap.

401 GRIERSON, HERBERT J. C. *Cross-Currents in Seventeenth Century English Literature: The World, The Flesh, and The Spirit, Their Actions and Reactions*. New York: Harper and Brothers, Harper Torchbooks TB47, 1958. 345 + xvi pp. Pap.

402 BROOKS, CLEANTH. *The Well Wrought Urn: Studies in the Structure of Poetry*. New York: Reynal and Hitchcock, [1947]. 270 + xi pp. W/o dj.

Last pages uncut.

Signed.

403 JOHNSON, SAMUEL. *Lives of the English Poets*. Introduction by

L. Archer-Hind. Vol.1, *Cowley to Prior*. Everyman's Library 770. London: J. M. Dent and Sons, 1954 (1779–81; London, 1925). 395 + xvi pp.

Marginal linings on pp. 70, 71, 77, 88, 93, 148. Underlining on p. 394.

Letters, pp. 26, 99, 214.

404 ————. *Lives of the English Poets*. Vol. 2, *Congreve to Gray*. Everyman's Library 771. London: J. M. Dent and Sons, 1953 (1779–81; London, 1925). 392 + v pp.

405 ARNOLD, MATTHEW. TRILLING, LIONEL. *Matthew Arnold*. New York: Meridian M19, 1955 (New York, 1939). 413 pp. Pap.

Marginal lining on p. 137.

"But there is a kind of situation which, though terrible, cannot give Joy—the situation in which 'a continuous state of mental distress is prolonged, unrelieved by incident, hope, or resistance; in which there is everything to be endured, nothing to be done.' A situation such as this is inevitably morbid, finding no vent in *action*. Human action is and always has been the material of true poetry; in Empedocles there is suffering but no relief in doing" (double marginal lining, p. 137).

406 HOPKINS, GERARD MANLEY. *Poems and Prose of Gerard Manley Hopkins*. Selected and ed., with introduction and notes, by W. H. Gardner. Harmondsworth, England: Penguin Poets D15, 1958 (1953) (London, 1948). 252 + xxxvi pp. Pap.

Letters, pp. 112, 517, 560, 586.

407 SEWELL, ELIZABETH. *Poems, 1947–1961*. Contemporary Poetry Series. Chapel Hill: University of North Carolina Press, [1962]. 76 pp.

Letters, p. 528.

408 YEATS, W. B. *The Collected Poems of W. B. Yeats*. New York: Macmillan, 1953 (1933). 480 + xv pp.

A few later pages uncut.

Signed, dated 1954.

409 BRANDES, GEORGE. *William Shakespeare.* Trans. William Archer, Mary Morison, and Diana White. New York: Macmillan, 1936. 721 + xii pp.

Signed photograph of Brandes pasted on flyleaf. "To Monsignor Dodwell with love. Jimmy. 'I'm the loneliest man in Denmark.' With best regards for your understanding and inspiration—Nena—" on the following page.

410 ELIOT, T. S. *Essays on Elizabethan Drama.* New York: Harcourt, Brace, Harvest HB18, [1956] [1932]. 178 + x pp. Pap.

411 CECIL, DAVID. *Early Victorian Novelists: Essays in Revaluation.* Harmondsworth, England: Penguin, Pelican A190, 1948 (1934). 253 pp. Pap.

Marginal lining on p. 45. Underlining on p. 33.

"It does not matter that Dickens' world is not lifelike: it is alive" (underlining, p. 33).

"If a writer's creative imagination only works within a limited range, it is clear he ought to stay within it. The great conscious artists, Jane Austen, Flaubert, and Turgenev, do; and this is why they are so consistently successful. There is a great deal they cannot write about; but they do not try" (marginal lining, p. 45).

412 MAISON, MARGARET M. *The Victorian Vision: Studies in the Religious Novel.* New York: Sheed and Ward, [1962]. 360 + ix pp.

Signed "F. O'Connor 1962."

Bulletin, 3.31.62; *Reviews,* p. 142.

413 CONRAD, JOSEPH. FORD, FORD MADOX. *Joseph Conrad: A Personal Remembrance.* London: Duckworth, 1924. 256 pp. Illus. W/o dj.

Signed "W. Limford Brown." Secondhand booksellers plate on inside front cover. Foxed.

Letters, p. 447.

414 FORD, FORD MADOX. GORDON, CAROLINE. *A Good Soldier: A Key to the Novels of Ford Madox Ford.* With a selective bibliography of works by and about Ford by Helmut E. Gerber. Uni-

versity of California Library at Davis, Chapbook no. 1. Davis: University of California, 1963. 31 + iii pp. Pap. Pamphlet. *Letters*, p. 534.

415 JOYCE, JAMES. ELLMANN, RICHARD. *James Joyce*. New York: Oxford University Press, 1959. 842 + xvi pp. Illus.

416 JOHNSON, SAMUEL. BOSWELL, JAMES. *The Life of Samuel Johnson*. Abridged edition with an introduction by Bergen Evans. New York: Modern Library 282, 1952. 559 + xv pp. W/o dj.

417 CARLYLE, THOMAS. *Collected Works of Thomas Carlyle*. Masterworks Library. New York: Greystone Press, n.d. 449 pp.
   Includes *Sartor Resartus, Heroes and Hero Worship*, and *Characteristics*.

418 CHESTERTON, G. K. *Lunacy and Letters*. Ed. Dorothy Collins. New York: Sheed and Ward. 1958. 192 pp.

419 HÖLDERLIN, FRIEDRICH. *Selected Poems of Friedrich Hölderlin*. Trans., with introduction and notes, by J. B. Leishman. London: Hogarth Press, 1954 (1944). 156 pp. Bilingual Edition.

420 CERF, BENNETT A., ED. *Great German Short Novels and Stories*. New York: Modern Library 108, [1933]. 475 + ix pp.

421 MANN, THOMAS. MANN, ERIKA. *The Last Year of Thomas Mann (Das Letzte Jahr)*. Trans. Richard Graves. New York: Farrar, Straus and Cudahy, 1958. 119 pp. Illus.

422 HELLER, ERICH. *The Disinherited Mind: Essays in Modern German Literature and Thought*. New York: Farrar, Straus and Cudahy, [1957]. 306 + xiv pp.
   Marginal linings, pp. 60, 138, 206. Underlining, p. 60.
   "For tragedy presupposes the belief in an external order of things which is indeed incomplete without the conformity of the human soul, but would be still more defective without the soul's freedom to violate it. Yet Faust's dilemma is different. His 'two souls' are merely the one soul divided in itself because it knows of no independent external reality to which it is related as a free agent. . . . Thus the

spiritual extremes of his existence are not guilt and atone-
ment, but despair and titanism. It is a situation unresolv-
able in tragedy" (complete marginal lining and underlining,
p. 60).

"It is astonishing and instructive to see how long an idea,
present right at the beginning of a poet's career, takes to
mature into great poetry" (marginal lining, p. 138).

". . . so deeply engrained is positivism in the critics of
this age that even when they are genuinely moved by the
symbolic reality which the author has created, they will
soon regain the balance of mind required for the translation
of the symbol into what it 'really' means; and by that they
mean precisely that meaningless experience which the artist
has succeeded in transcending through his poetic creation"
(marginal lining, p. 206).

"In Kafka we have before us the modern mind, seem-
ingly self-sufficient, intelligent, sceptical, ironical, splen-
didly trained for the great game of pretending that the
world it comprehends in sterilized sobriety is the only and
ultimate reality there is—yet a mind living in sin with the
soul of Abraham" (marginal lining, p. 206).

Letters, p. 334.

423 IBSEN, HENRIK. *A Doll's House, Ghosts, An Enemy of the
People,* and *The Master Builder.* Introduction by Eric Bentley.
New York: Modern Library 6, [1950]. 383 + xxiv pp.

424 MAURIAC, FRANÇOIS. *Great Men.* Trans. Elsie Pell. London:
Rockliff, n.d. (Monaco, 1949). 127 + vii pp. Illus.

425 POULET, GEORGES. *Studies in Human Time (Etudes sur le temps
humain).* Trans. Elliott Coleman. New York: Harper and
Brothers, Harper Torchbooks, Academy Library TB 1004,
1959 (Baltimore, 1956). 363 + ix pp. Pap.

Marginal lining on p. vii of preface. Check mark on p.
15.

"The author conceives the essential effort of the critic to
be that of discerning the total meaning of a writer's work by

paying attention to his sense of man's temporality and place. Once this is understood, in relation to all other human activity, then the philosophic temper of the literature of a time is seen as vitally determining the way life will take. The work of an artist can be penetrated and can penetrate us, unhindered, only if we are led to a view of the center of it, where the generative power is imparted. Without this second sight, works of art can hardly be seen or known at all" (marginal lining, page [vii]: translator's preface).

426 FOWLIE, WALLACE, *The Spirit of France: Studies in Modern French Literature.* London: Sheed and Ward, 1945 (1944). 138 + vi pp.

427 VILLON, FRANÇOIS. *The Ballades and Lyrics of François Villon.* Trans. John Payne, Dante Gabriel Rossetti, Algernon Charles Swinburne, Andrew Lang, and William Ernest Henley. Mount Vernon, N.Y.: Peter Pauper Press, n.d. 60 pp. Boxed.

    Signed, dated 1945.

428 MOLIÈRE, JEAN BAPTISTE POQUELIN. *Plays.* Introduction by Francis Fergusson. New York: Modern Library 78, [1950]. 364 pp.

429 PHAEDRA AND FIGARO. RACINE, JEAN BAPTISTE. *Phaedra and Figaro. Phaedra.* Trans., with a preface, by Robert Lowell. BEAUMARCHAIS, PIERRE AUGUSTIN CARON DE. *Figaro's Marriage.* Trans., with a preface, by Jacques Barzun. New York: Farrar, Straus and Cudahy, [1961]. 213 pp. Illus.

430 BRUCKBERGER, RAYMOND-LÉOPOLD, DOMINICAIN. *Madeleine et Judas: Tragédie en Trois Mystères* (Magdalene and Judas: A Tragedy in Three Mysteries). [N.p., 1956.] 158 pp. Pap. In French.

    Number 301 in a limited edition of 500 copies.

    Letters, p. 222.

431 TURNELL, MARTIN. *The Novel in France.* New York: Vintage K-62, 1958 (New York, 1951). 447 + xiv + vii pp. Pap.

    Letters, p. 356.

432 MONTAIGNE, MICHEL DE. *Selected Essays*. Trans., with an introduction and notes, by Donald M. Frame. Classics Club. New York: Walter J. Black, [1943]. 364 + xxx pp. W/o plasticine wrap.

Signed "M. F. O'Connor—1943." Brackets on pp. 6, 12, 17, 18. Check marks on pp. 20, 24, 33.

433 BERNANOS, GEORGES. *The Last Essays of Georges Bernanos*. Trans. Joan Ulanov and Barry Ulanov. Chicago: Henry Regnery, [1955]. 263 + vi pp.

434 RABELAIS, FRANÇOIS. LEWIS, D. B. WYNDAM. *Doctor Rabelais*. New York: Sheed and Ward, [1957]. 274 pp.

Marginal lining on pp. 129, 147, 253, 254. Check mark on p. 51.

Bulletin, 12.21.57; *Reviews*, pp. 46–47; *Letters*, p. 241.

435 PÉGUY, CHARLES. *Temporal and Eternal*. Trans. Alexander Dru. New York: Harper and Brothers, [1958] (Paris, 1955). 159 pp.

An adaptation of *Notre Jeunesse*, 1910, and of *Clio I*.

Marginal linings on pp. 22–23, 50, 64, 65, 103, 117.

Bulletin, 1.10.59; *Reviews*, p. 66.

436 MAURIAC, FRANÇOIS. *Mémoires Interieures*. Trans. Gerard Hopkins. New York: Farrar, Straus and Cudahy, 1961. 248 pp.

"E. Brontë 61ff" on dj. Marginal lining on pp. 117–18.

"Here I touch on what, to my mind, gives so great a value to *The Scarlet Letter*. This book furnishes us with a key to what seems the most impenetrable of all mysteries, especially to the believer: the mystery of evil. Evil is in the world, and in ourselves. Yet, 'all is Grace.' Those are the last words of Bernanos's country priest. The very principle of our regeneration is to be found in what is worst in us. From this point of view, *The Scarlet Letter* is a document of supreme importance which I have frequently brought to the attention of the troubled and despairing. In it we are shown a guilty pastor who passes for a saint: 'To the high mountain peaks of faith and sanctity he would have climbed, had not the tendency been thwarted by the burden, whatever it might be, of crime or anguish, beneath which it was his doom to totter. It kept him down on the level of the lowest; him, the man of ethereal attributes, whose voice the angels might have listened to and answered! But this very burden it was that gave him sympathies so intimate with the sinful brotherhood of mankind: so that his heart vibrated in unison with theirs, and sent its throb of pain through a thousand other hearts. . . .' What follows, must be read in its entirety.

"It is not only because he humiliates himself, because he sees his own objection and beats his breast, that the guilty pastor draws near to God: his very sin becomes in him a principle of total renewal before his brethren, but also before God. Similarly, the scarlet letter fastened to the breast of the young woman guilty of adultery, makes of her, in the eyes of the whole town, an authentic and venerated saint. What we are shown is pharisaism transmuted into the creative element of sanctity. Grace turns to its own purposes the worst canalizations invented by Tartuffe and Orgon. Its waters flow through them to reach and fertilize the hearts of men. The spirit makes use of the letter, no matter how despicable the letter may be. That is the moral of this sombre tale.

"Some may hold that a novel which interests us mainly because of its theological implications can scarcely claim any very considerable degree of importance from the literary point of view. But the fact that, in spite of an outmoded technique, it still, after a century, has so great a power of suggestion, does, so it seems to me, bear witness to the richness of a literary form on which certain modern practitioners would impose their own narrow code. The genuine novel can afford to laugh at their 'art of fiction' just as the genuine poet can laugh at 'the art of poetry.' A novel can express anything and everything, and can achieve, as does *The Scarlet Letter*, the remarkable triumph of turning a cruel caricature of Christian-

ity into an apologia which opens a door upon the mystery of
evil" (marginal lining, pp. 117–18).

Letters, p. 431.

437 DANTE ALIGHIERI. *The Divine Comedy of Dante Alighieri.*
Trans. John Aitken Carlyle and P. H. Wicksteed. Introduction by C. H. Grandgent. New York: Modern Library 208,
[1932]. 625 + xix pp. Illus. W/o dj.

Signed, dated 1946. Probably used as a school text. Marginal linings on pp. 13, 20, 23, 25, 37, 42, 47, 53, 54, 60, 73, 77,
141, 145, 169, 172, 182, 224, 225, 285, 316, 348, 403, 417, 434,
485, 580. Underlinings on pp. 18, 22, 23, 27, 29, 31, 36, 37, 42,
45, 47, 50, 51, 55, 56, 60, 61, 62, 72, 73, 77, 141, 145, 178, 196,
217, 223, 224, 416, 417, 434, 485, 564, 580. Check marks on
pp. 43, 201, 217, 223, 306, 314, 327, 345. Arrows on pp. 38, 46.
Marginalia: "Beatrice," p. 14; "virtue—reason," p. 22;
"sinned in life so *God* has *willed* that they shall sin after life—
They sin without remorse—only want to sin more," p. 25;
"Last Judgment," p. 38; "Christ," p. 38; "wolf—papal
power—clergy avarice Guelphs (Popes party)," p. 40;
"misers & spendthrifts," p. 40; "fortune acts according to
God," p. 42; "To Dante—highest virtue was proportion in all
things (?)," p. 43; "enemy of Dantes," p. 45; "imp.," p. 47;
"Act I," p. 47; "Act II," p. 48; "Act III," p. 49; "Act III," p. 50;
"inadequacy of man alone," p. 51; "mythical drama between
hell & heaven," p. 51; "Act IV," p. 51; "Divine salvation
effected," p. 51; "no real power in hell," p. 51; "deepening of
consciousness of sin comes with this rescue," p. 51; "uses
Epicureans because they didn't believe in imortality—their
tombs symbolize a living death—in and after life," p. 54;
"voluntary unbelievers," p. 54; "demands intellect," p. 61;
"blasphemy suicide murder," p. 61; "blasphemy worse than
murder," p. 61; "the official speaking," p. 72; "envy," p. 73;
"struggle between St. Frances & the devil illustrates the
struggle between good intentions & actual deeds," p. 147;
"ice—isolation—freezing of the soul by trechery," p. 165;

"Ugolino betrayed his own city, Pisa," p. 174; "in particular," p. 175; "died of hunger not sorrow," p. 177; "Ugolino—
(1) the sorrowful father (2) the bitter hater of the bishop," p.
180; "hatred impotence ignorance," p. 182; "In hell—an ex-
emplification of hell as everlasting punishment. Without
free-will you could not have hell as Christian conceives it—
pagan doesn't blame man as much since man is not wholly to
blame for his sins. State of hell is a state of rebellion against
the divine order. Sinner in hell contradicts his own reason—
against society also," p. 185; "sinner in hell becomes more
bitter rather than repentant if he realized that he was respon-
sible for his position he would be in purgatory—where the
pain would purify his soul," p. 186; "Fuller Martin Russel,"
p. 191; "Cato serves as symbol for the whole purgatory represents moral law as he had represented social law on earth,"
p. 196; "4 cardinal virtues," p. 196; "symbol of humility," p.
197; "Casella," p. 201; "escaping bondage of sin," p. 203;
"Pride Envy Anger) sins of perversion (love) Sloth—defective love Averice Gluttony Carnality) excessive love," p. 205;
"Buconte da Montefeltro son of Guido," p. 217; "Sardello,"
p. 223; "imp.!" p. 285; "Hugh Capet," p. 306; "Statius," p.
314; "Forese Donati," p. 327; "Guido Guinicelli," p. 345;
"needn't say 'lead us into temptation' because souls in Purgatory are not tempted," p. 348; "not to the same degree," p.
403; "essence of injustice," p. 564; "In Paradise each man
finds his proper place," p. 565.
    Letters, p. 116.

438 DAVENPORT, BASIL, ED. *The Portable Roman Reader*. Introduc-
    tion by Davenport. New York: Viking Press, Viking Por-
    table Library P56, 1959 (1951). 656 + xi pp. Pap.

439 HORACE. *Selected Poems of Horace*. Introduction by George F.
    Whicher. Classics Club College Edition. New York: D. Van
    Nostrand, [1947]. 284 + xxvii pp.

440 THE BESTIARY. WHITE, T. H., ED. AND TRANS. *The Bestiary: A
    Book of Beasts, being a translation from a Latin Bestiary of the*

Twelfth Century. New York: G. P. Putnam's Sons, Capricorn Cap 26, 1960 (New York, 1954). [296] pp. Illus.

441 ARISTOPHANES. *The Birds.* Trans. Dudley Fitts. New York: Harcourt, Brace, [1957]. 181 + viii pp.

442 ———. *The Frogs.* Trans. Dudley Fitts. New York: Harcourt, Brace, [1955]. 166 + xii pp.

443 GRENE, DAVID, AND RICHMOND LATTIMORE, EDS. *The Complete Greek Tragedies.* 4 vols. Vol. 1, *Aeschylus;* vol. 2, *Sophocles;* vol. 3, *Euripides;* vol. 4, *Euripides.* Chicago: University of Chicago Press, 1959. [351] + viii pp.; [460] + vi pp.; [661] + x pp.; [616] + vi pp. Decorations. Boxed set.

    Letters, p. 378.

444 SOPHOCLES. *The Oedipus Cycle.* With commentaries. *Oedipus Rex,* trans. Dudley Fitts and Robert Fitzgerald. *Oedipus at Colonus,* trans. Robert Fitzgerald. *Antigone,* trans. Dudley Fitts and Robert Fitzgerald. New York: Harcourt, Brace, Harvest HB8 [1949] [1939]. 243 pp. Pap.

    Letters, pp. 16, 50, 68, 111, 267, 530.

445 ———. *Oedipus Rex.* Trans. Dudley Fitts and Robert Fitzgerald. New York: Harcourt, Brace, 1949. 109 pp.

    "To Flannery from Robert, September 1949" on flyleaf.

446 HOMER. *The Odyssey.* Trans. Robert Fitzgerald. Drawings by Hans Erni. Garden City, N.Y.: Doubleday, 1961. 474 pp.

    "With love to Flannery and Regina at the farm April 3, 1961. Robert Fitzgerald" on flyleaf. Fitzgerald has corrected "pretelling" to "forecasting," p. 101, and corrected typographical errors in colophon, p. [475].

    Letters, pp. 62, 66, 122, 127, 138, 267, 336, 530.

447 KAZANTZAKIS, NIKOS. *The Odyssey: A Modern Sequel.* Trans., with an introduction, synopsis, and notes, by Kimon Friar. Illustrations by Ghika. New York: Simon and Schuster, 1958. 824 + xxxviii pp.

    Letters, p. 310.

448 TURGENEV, IVAN. *Three Famous Plays: A Month in the Country, A Provincial Lady,* and *A Poor Gentleman.* Trans. Constance Garnett. Introduction by David Garnett. New York: Hill

and Wang, Mermaid Dramabook MD15, 1959. 235 + xii pp. Pap.

449 GOGOL, NIKOLAI. NABOKOV, VLADIMIR. *Nikolai Gogol.* The Makers of Modern Literature. Norfolk, Conn.: New Directions 78, [1944]. 172 pp. Pap. Illus.

450 TURGENEV, IVAN. *Literary Reminiscences and Autobiographical Fragments.* Trans., with an introduction, by David Magarshack. Essay on Turgenev by Edmund Wilson. New York: Farrar, Straus and Cudahy, 1958. 309 pp.

451 POLISH SHORT STORIES. Ed. Jadwiga Lewicka. Selected by Zbigniew Zabicki. Warsaw: Polonia Publishing, 1960. [324] pp. Illus. In English.

Anthology. Some last pages uncut.

452 JAPANESE HAIKU. BASHO, BUSON, ISSA, SHIKI, SOKAN, KIKAYU, CHIYO-NI, JOSO, YAHA, BONCHO, AND OTHERS. *Japanese Haiku.* Mount Vernon, N.Y.: Peter Pauper Press, [1956]. [55] pp. Decorations.

453 O'CONNOR, FLANNERY. *The Artificial Nigger and Other Tales.* London: Neville Spearman, 1957. 251 pp.

The English edition of *A Good Man Is Hard to Find.* This book is stored separately in the O'Connor Room with the journals and magazines.

Signed "Flannery O'Connor Milledgeville, Georgia" on flyleaf. For "A Good Man Is Hard to Find": brackets, p. 12, lines 10–13; underlining of "one" and "only," p. 17, line 32; text corrections, "and faced" changed to "toward," p. 9, line 16; "she" changed to "the grandmother," p. 12, line 16; "nigger" changed to "colored," p. 13, line 19.

Letters, pp. 249–50.

History

454 D'ARCY, M. C., S.J. *The Meaning and Matter of History: A Christian View.* New York: Farrar, Straus and Cudahy, [1959]. 309 pp.

Written on front dj: "114 Toynbee." Marginal linings, pp. 195, 197, 255. Marginalia: "Pirandello?" p. 28.

"It is the 'time of our visitation.' All life is an expectancy, the tense awaiting for the knock on the door and the sound of a voice saying: 'It is I'; and because this Coming is decisive and felt to be final, it is described by apocalyptic writers in terms of judgment, sudden call, catastrophic change, ultimate separation or union, and it is localized in the coming of faith and grace, the Church, death, the passing of a generation and the last assize" (marginal lining, p. 195).

"And no wonder; for Thou hast 'thy dark descending and most art merciful then' " (marginal lining, p. 197).

455 DAWSON, CHRISTOPHER. *The Dynamics of World History.* Ed. John J. Mulloy. New York: New American Library, Mentor Omega MQ378, 1962 (New York, 1956). 477 + xii pp. Pap.

456 VOEGELIN, ERIC. *Order and History.* 6 vols. Vol. 1, *Israel and Revelation.* Baton Rouge: Louisiana State University Press, 1956. 533 + xxv pp.

Signed, dated 1958. Marginal linings on pp. 123, 124, 125, 125–26, 126, 127, 129, 130, 133, 140, 145, 300, 315–16, 339, 357, 368, 369, 409, 410, 440, 460, 483, 485, 491. Brackets, p. 385. Underlinings on pp. 125, 133, 155, 314, 315, 320, 409, 429. Check mark on p. 385. Marginalia: "the peacock," p. 320.

"History, we therefore conclude, is a symbolic form of existence, of the same class as the cosmological form; and the paradigmatic narrative is, in the historical form, the equivalent of the myth in the cosmological form. Hence it will be necessary to distinguish between political societies according to their form of existence: the Egyptian society existed in cosmological, the Israelite in historical form" (marginal lining, p. 124).

"The inclusion of the past in history through retrospective interpretation is not an 'arbitrary' or 'subjective' construction but the genuine discovery of a process which, though its goal is unknown to the generations of the past, leads in continuity into the historical present. The historical present is differentiated in a process that is itself historical in so far as the compact symbolism gradually loosens up until the historical truth contained in it emerges in articulate form" (marginal lining, p. 129).

"Now, historical form, understood as the experience of the present under God, will appear as subjective only, if faith is misinterpreted as a 'subjective' experience. If, however, it is understood as the leap in being, as the entering of the soul into divine reality through the entering of divine reality into the soul, the historical form, far from being a subjective point of view, is an ontologically real event in history. And it must be understood as an event of this nature, as long as we base our conception of history on a critical analysis of the literary sources which report the event and do not introduce subjectivity ourselves by arbitrary, ideological surmising. If now the men to whom it happens explicate the meaning of the event through symbols, the explication will cast an ordering ray of objective truth over the field of history in which the event objectively occurred" (marginal lining, p. 130).

"The Israelite conception of true order in the human soul, in society, and in history cannot be ascertained through consultation of treatises which explicitly deal with such subject matters. The historical narrative from the creation of the world to the fall of Jerusalem is neither a book, nor a collection of books, but a unique symbolism that has grown into its ultimate form through more than six centuries of historiographic work from the time of Solomon to *ca.* 300 B.C." (marginal lining, p. 145).

"Here was a people that began its existence in history with a radical leap in being; and only after the people had been constituted by that initial experience did it acquire, in the course of centuries, a mundane body of organization to sustain itself in existence. This sequence, reversing the ordinary course of social evolution, is unique in history. It is so unbelievable that positivist historians, as for instance Eduard Meyer, do not believe it at all. . . . A society is supposed to start from primitive rites and myths, and thence to advance gradually, if at all, to the spirituality of a transcendent religion; it is not supposed to start where a respectable society has difficulties even ending. Nevertheless, the mystery of Israel's start at the wrong end of evolution must be accepted, the progressive thesis that first things come always first notwithstanding. In this one case the sequence actually was reversed; and the reversal was the cause of Israel's extraordinary creativity in the realm of symbols" (underlining, p. 315; marginal lining, pp. 315–16).

"abbreviated cosmos" (underlined, quoting Philo, annotated "the peacock," p. 320).

"The disciples, however, began to wonder. The Son of God was with them. Why, then, should the scribes say that first Elijah must come? (17:10). The question was answered by Jesus in the Logion 17:11–12: 'Elijah does come, and he is to restore [*apokatastasei*] all things. / But I say unto you: Elijah has come already, / And they did not recognize him, and did to him at their will. / And in like manner the Son of Man will suffer at their hands.' The Logion is followed by the Evangelist's information that only then the disciples understood Jesus was speaking to them about John the Baptist (17:13)" (marginal lining, p. 339).

"For the detail of pragmatic events is of little interest" (bracketed with marginal check mark, p. 385).

"They can make their assumption, second, because they remain unaware that the revelation creates history as the inner form of human existence in the present under God" (marginal lining and partly underlined, p. 409).

"The prophets were faced with the task of reformulating the problem of history in such a manner that the empirical Israel of their time could disappear from the scene without destroying by its disappearance the order of history as created by revelation" (marginal lining, p. 460).

Bulletin, 11.15.58; *Reviews*, pp. 60–61; *Letters*, pp. 294–95.

457 ———. *Order and History*. Vol. 2, *The World of the Polis*. Baton Rouge: Louisiana State University Press, [1957]. 389 + xviii pp.

Signed, dated 1958. O'Connor's numbers on back dj: "6 28 51 72 74 103 126 127 156 170 241 263 281." Marginal linings on pp. 6, 7, 8, 28, 49, 51, 67, 72–73, 74, 76, 103, 108, 126, 127, 156, 157–58, 170, 192, 237, 241, 263, 264, 274, 281. Underlinings on pp. 7, 68, 71, 74, 75, 104, 127, 241, 263, 274, 281. Check mark on p. 3. S signs on pp. 13, 23, 24.

"The leap in being entails the obligations to communicate and to listen. Revelation and response are not a man's private affair; for the revelation comes to one man for all men, and in his response he is the representative of mankind. And since the response is representative it endows the recipient of revelation, in relation to his fellow men, with the authority of the prophet" (marginal lining, p. 6).

"The Homeric problems of order originate in the uncertainties concerning the nature of man. Only one thing is really certain even about Homeric man: he must die. Hence, 'mortal' is the preferred synonym for man, distinguishing his nature without a doubt from that of the immortal gods. For the rest, the transhuman elements of the order of being penetrate so deeply into man or, from the other side, man is yet so imperfectly closed as a self-conscious, reflecting agent, that the status of various phenomena as human or divine must remain in doubt and, in particular, that quite frequently it will not be certain to what extent the actions of man are his actions at all. Homer's difficulties in dealing with these problems, as well as the importance of his partial solutions, can be understood only if we place ourselves in his position. If, on the contrary, we interpret the epics under the assumption that he knew already what gods and men were, his specific achievement in clarifying the nature of man and the meaning of order will be obscured" (marginal lining, p. 103).

". . . and the hero in the Homeric sense can be defined as the man in whose actions a more-than-human order of being becomes manifest" (underlining, p. 104).

"The Homeric achievement is remarkable as a struggle for the understanding of the psyche with the rather crude symbols that we have studied. Homer astutely observed that the disorder of a society was a disorder in the soul of its component members, and especially in the soul of the ruling class. The symptoms of the disease were magnificently described by the great poet; but the true genius of the great thinker revealed itself in the creation of a tentative psychology without the aid of an adequate conceptual apparatus" (marginal lining, p. 108).

"The speculative reason of the thinker asserts its autonomy against the mythopoetic mode of expression" (double marginal lining, p. 126).

"The course of human affairs becomes a course of history when the order of the soul becomes the ordering force of society. For only then can the rise and fall of a polity be experienced in terms of a growing or disintegrating psyche" (marginal lining, p. 263).

Bulletin, 1.24.59; *Reviews*, pp. 67–68; *Letters*, pp. 310, 316.

458 ———. *Order and History*. Vol. 3, *Plato and Aristotle*. Baton Rouge: Louisiana State University Press, [1957]. 383 + xvii pp.

Signed, dated 1959. O'Connor's numbers on dj: "34 37 63 69 92 96 116–128 133 161 164fol 186 203 221 226 261 284 290 364"; "355 play & leisure" on back dj. Marginal linings on pp. 5, 11, 34–35, 37, 63, 69, 70, 92, 96, 115–16, 128, 129, 133, 161, 169, 170, 174, 186, 188, 193, 203, 221–22, 226, 227, 245, 261, 264, 265, 276, 278, 284, 288, 291–92, 355, 356, 364. Underlinings on pp. 11, 12, 170. Check marks on pp. 163, 179. Marginalia: "Buber," p. 12; "St Thomas," p. 285.

"The dialogue is the symbolic form of the order of wisdom, in opposition to the oration as the symbolic form of the disordered society" (underlined, with the annotation "Buber," p. 12).

"Without change of terminology, through a slight switch from metaphor to reality, the inquiry into the paradigm of a good polis is revealed as an inquiry into man's existence in a community that lies, not only beyond the polis, but beyond any political order in history. The leap in being, toward the transcendent source of order, is real in Plato; and later ages have recognized rightly in the passage a prefiguration of St. Augustine's conception of the *civitas Dei*" (marginal lining, p. 92).

"The soul may become the scene on which a drama is enacted" (check mark, p. 179).

"The myth remains the legitimate expression of the fundamental movements of the soul. Only in the shelter of the myth can the sectors of the personality that are closer to the waking consciousness unfold their potentiality; and without the ordering of the whole personality by the truth of the myth the secondary intellectual and moral powers would lose their direction. It is, on principle, the insight that has found its classic expression in the Anselmian *credo ut intelligam*" (marginal lining, p. 186).

"The symbols of the myth are translated into realities and aims of anthropomorphic man: The nature of man is basically good; the source of evils is to be found in the institutions; organization and revolution can abolish such evils as still exist; the powers of man can create a society free from want and fear; the ideas of infinite perfectibility, of the superman, and of self-salvation make their appearance" (marginal lining, p. 188).

". . . the Church infuses as much of its substance as men are capable of absorbing while living in the world; the mediation of the stark reality of Jesus to the level of human expediency, with a minimum loss of substance, is one of the functions of the Church" (double marginal lining, p. 226).

Bulletin, 5.2.59; *Reviews,* pp. 70–71.

459 ORTEGA Y GASSET, JOSÉ. *The Revolt of the Masses (La Rebelión de las Masas).* Authorized anonymous trans. New York: New American Library, Mentor M49, 1952 (1930; New York, 1932). 141 pp. Pap.

Broken spine.

460 TOYNBEE, ARNOLD J. *A Study of History.* Abridgment of vols. 1–6 by D. C. Somervell. New York: Oxford University Press, 1947 (1946). 617 + xiii pp. W/o dj.

Signed, dated 1947.

461 WEAVER, RICHARD M. *Ideas Have Consequences.* Chicago: University of Chicago Press, Phoenix P44, 1960 (Chicago, 1948). [190]. + vii pp. Pap.

462 JAMES, HENRY. *The American Scene, Together with Three Essays from "Portraits of Places."* Ed., with an introduction, by W. H. Auden. New York: Charles Scribner's Sons, 1946. 520 + xxx pp. Illus.

Signed, dated 1954. Marginal linings on pp. 423, 471, 477. Check marks, p. 423.

"I think of the inimitable detachment with which, at the very moment he spoke, the negro porter engaged at the door of the conveyance put straight down into the mud of the road the dressing-bag I was obliged, a few minutes later, in our close-pressed company, to nurse on my knees; and I go so far, even, as almost to lose myself in the sense of other occasions evoked by that reminiscence; this marked anomaly, the apparently deep-seated inaptitude of the negro race at large for any alertness of personal service, having been throughout a lively surprise" (marginal lining and check marks, p. 423).

Letters, p. 462.

463 SIMKINS, FRANCIS BUTLER. *The Everlasting South.* Foreword
by Charles P. Roland. Baton Rouge: Louisiana State University Press, [1963]. 103 + xv pp.

Signed, dated 1964.

464 CASH, W. J. *The Mind of the South.* Garden City, N.Y.: Doubleday, Anchor A27, 1954 [New York, 1941]. 444 pp. Pap.

Marginal linings on pp. 99, 101, 103. Marginalia: "still is,"
p. 103; "still does," p. 103.

"The final result of conflict and solidification, we have to
notice, is that it turned the South toward strait-jacket conformity and made it increasingly intolerant of dissent. Perhaps, in view of Southern individualism, this seems para-
doxical and even contradictory. The right to dissent, one
might think, is the very sap and life of individualism. But in
fact there is no real contradiction here, or none that was not
inherent in the South itself.

"We go back to the point that it was the individualism of
extremely simple men, shaped by what were basically very
simple and homogeneous conditions. The community and
uniformity of origins, the nearness in time of the frontier,
the failure of immigration and the growth of important
towns—all these co-operated to cut men to a single pattern,
and, as we have been seeing continuously, the total effect of
the plantation world was to bind them to a single focus
which was held with peculiar intensity" (marginal lining, p.
99).

Letters, p. 225.

465 LONGSTREET, A. B. *Georgia Scenes: Characters, Incidents, Etc.,
in the First Half Century of the Republic.* General editor, Louis
M. Hacker. Introduction by B. R. McElderry, Jr. American
Century Series S-24. New York: Sagamore Press, 1957. 198
+ x pp. Pap.

466 BISHOP, ELIZABETH. MORLEY, HELENA. *The Diary of "Helena
Morley."* Ed. and trans., with an introduction, by Bishop.

New York: Farrar, Straus and Cudahy, 1957. 281 + xxxvii pp. Illus.

A girlhood journal of life in a mountain town of Brazil at the turn of the century.

"This book is sent with the compliments of The Author," on enclosed slip. Signed, verso of flyleaf.

Letters, p. 265.

467 CALL, HUGHIE. *The Little Kingdom*. Illustrations by Gloria Kamen. Boston: Houghton Mifflin, 1964. 134 pp. Illus.

A children's book.

468 ADAMS, HENRY. *The Education of Henry Adams*. Introduction by James Truslow Adams. New York: Modern Library 76, [1931] [1918]. 517 + x pp. W/o dj.

Signed "M. F. O'Connor" on flyleaf. Marginal linings on pp. 78, 85. Underlining, p. 78.

469 ALLEN, FREDERICK LEWIS. *A Register of His Papers in the Library of Congress*. Washington, D.C.: Library of Congress, Reference Dept., Manuscript Div., 1958. 7 pp. Pap.

470 TACITUS. *The Complete Works*. Ed., with an introduction, by Moses Hadas. Trans. Alfred John Church and William Jackson Brodribb. New York: Modern Library 222, [1942]. 773 + [xxvi] pp.

Letters, pp. 150, 161–62.

471 GOLDSMITH, DR. *Pinnock's Improved Edition of Dr. Goldsmith's History of Greece, for the Use of Schools*. 35th American, from 19th English, ed. Philadelphia: Thomas, Cowperthwait, 1851. 380 pp. Illus. W/o dj.

Foxed pages. Loose spine.

472 HERODOTUS. *The Histories*. Trans., with an introduction, by Aubrey de Sélincourt. Penguin Classics L34. Harmondsworth, England: Penguin, 1959 (Harmondsworth, 1954). [602] pp. Pap. Maps.

473 TOCQUEVILLE, ALEXIS DE. *The Old Régime and the French Revolution (L'Ancien régime et la revolution)*. Trans. Stuart Gilbert. Garden City, N.Y.: Doubleday, Anchor A60, 1955 (1856). 300 + xv pp. Pap.

474 PAYNE, JOHN HOWARD. *John Howard Payne to His Country-men.* Ed., with an introduction, by Clemens de Baillou. University of Georgia Libraries Miscellanea Publications, no. 2. Athens: University of Georgia Press, 1961. 61 + v pp. Pamphlet. Pap.

"To Miss Flannery O'Connor in admiration. [?] Baillou" on flyleaf.

475 HOCKETT, HOMER CAREY. *Political and Social Growth of the American People: 1492–1865.* 3d ed. New York: Macmillan, 1943 (New York, 1940). 861 + xxi pp. Illus. Maps. W/o dj.

New ed. of *Political and Social Growth of the United States, 1492–1852.*

Signed "M. F. O'Connor, Milledgeville Georgia" on flyleaf; a school text. Underlining, p. 562. Check marks, pp. 592, 630, 847. Summary notes from text on last blank page are possibly not in O'Connor's hand. Checked in index: Albany Plan of Union; Joseph Galloway; Galloway Plan; New England Confederation.

"Nor is it to be overlooked that this election marked the first widespread use of campaign cartoons. By means of this shrewd and sometimes grotesque symbolism, political parties found it possible to instruct countless voters whose interest could have been excited in no other way" (underlining, p. 562).

476 SANDBURG, CARL. *A Lincoln Preface.* New York: Harcourt, Brace, 1954. 16 pp.

"This first edition is limited to twenty-eight hundred and fifty copies privately printed for the friends of the author and his publishers as a New Year's greeting."

477 BARUCH, BERNARD M. *Baruch: The Public Years.* New York: Holt, Rinehart and Winston, [1960]. 431 + xii pp. Illus.

478 WOODWARD, C. VANN. *The Burden of Southern History.* Baton Rouge: Louisiana State University Press, [1960]. 205 + xiv pp.

Signed, dated 1963. Marginal lining on p. 146.

Letters, p. 522.

479 ———. *Origins of the New South: 1877–1913.* Vol. 9 of *A History of the South,* ed. Wendell Holmes Stephenson and E. Merton Coulter. Baton Rouge and Austin: Louisiana State University Press and the Littlefield Fund for Southern History of the University of Texas, 1962 (1951). 542 + xi pp. Illus.

Signed, dated 1964. Marginal linings on pp. 155, 157, 164, 166. Marginal marking on p. 139. Underlining on p. 156.

"The Southern people remained, throughout the rise of the 'New South,' overwhelmingly a country people, by far the most rural section of the Union" (marginal marking, p. 139).

"In 1885, the year Page left for New York, Cable published *The Silent South,* the most radical indictment of Southern racial policy written by a Southerner in that period, and in 1885 he moved his family to Northampton, Massachusetts. He had the right, as he said, to speak as 'a native of Louisiana, an ex-Confederate soldier, and a lover of my home, my city, and my State.' Yet he never again lived in the South. Both Cable and his people were losers—the writer, of his art, which never fulfilled its rich promise; the South, of a fearless critic and a point of view that could thenceforth be more readily dismissed complacently as foreign. Later Cable would look homeward and melt with ruth: 'I felt that I belonged still,' he wrote, 'peculiarly to the South' " (last part of marginal lining, p. 164).

480 BONNER, JAMES C. *The Georgia Story.* Oklahoma City–Chattanooga: Harlow Publishing, 1958. 492 + xii pp. Illus. W/o dj.

Appendices. Bonner was a professor of history at Georgia State College for Women, Milledgeville. O'Connor is discussed, p. 459.

"For Flannery O'Connor with sincere appreciation. James C. Bonner Oct. 23, 1958" on flyleaf.

Letters, p. 300.

481 BRYAN, T. CONN. *Confederate Georgia.* Athens: University of Georgia Press, [1953]. 299 + x pp.

Bryan is a native of Milledgeville and taught at Georgia Military College there.

"To Flannery O'Connor, With regards, T. Conn Bryan May 16, 1953" on flyleaf.

482 JACKSON, JAMES. HAWES, LILLA M., ED. *The Papers of James Jackson, 1781–1798.* Vol. 9 of *Collections of the Georgia Historical Society.* Savannah: Georgia Historical Society, 1955. 110 pp.

483 KEELER, CLYDE E. *Land of the Moon-Children: The Primitive San Blas Culture in Flux.* Athens: University of Georgia Press, 1956. 207 + x pp. Illus.

Keeler was a professor of biology at Georgia State College for Women, Milledgeville.

"For Flannery O'Connor. Clyde Keeler, Dec. 14, 1956" on flyleaf.

Fiction

484 AMIS, KINGSLEY. *Lucky Jim.* New York: Viking Press, Compass C-35, 1958 [New York, 1953]. 256 pp. Pap.

Signed on front cover.

Letters, pp. 284, 301.

485 ANDERSON, SHERWOOD. *Winesburg, Ohio: A Group of Tales of Ohio Small-town Life.* Introduction by Ernest Boyd. New York: Modern Library 104, [1947] [1919]. 303 + xv pp.

Signed, dated 1960.

486 BABEL, ISAAC. *The Collected Stories.* Ed. and trans. Walter Morison. Introduction by Lionel Trilling. New York: Meridian MF3, 1960 [1929]. 381 pp. Pap.

Enclosed card reads "Mr. Roger Williams Straus, Jr."

487 BEDFORD, SYBILLE. *A Legacy.* New York: Simon and Schuster, 1957 [1956]. 311 pp.

488 BEERBOHM, MAX. *Seven Men and Two Others.* New York: Vintage K80, 1959 [New York, 1920]. 185 pp. Pap.

489 ———. *Zuleika Dobson.* Introduction by Francis Hackett. New York: Modern Library 116, [1926] [New York, 1911]. 358 + xi pp.

490 BERNANOS, GEORGES. *The Diary of a Country Priest.* Trans. Pamela Morris. Garden City, N.Y.: Doubleday, Image D6, 1960 (1954) (New York, 1937) (Paris, n.d.). 232 pp. Pap.

"For Flannery on Valentine's day. My love, Roslyn. (We've just been studying this in Fiction—thought you might like it, too)" on inside front cover.

Letters, pp. 98, 231, 296, 304, 306, 570.

491 ———. Copy 2. 1957 printing.

492 ———. *Joy.* Trans. Louise Varèse. New York: Pantheon, [1946]. [297] pp.

Signed.

493 BEYLE, MARIE-HENRI (STENDHAL). *The Charterhouse of Parma.* Trans. C. K. Scott-Moncrieff. Garden City, N.Y.: Doubleday, Anchor A1, 1953 (New York, 1925; Paris, 1839). 510 pp. Pap.

494 ———. *The Red and the Black.* Trans. C. K. Scott-Moncrieff. New York: Modern Library 157, n.d. [New York, 1926]. [350] + iv pp. W/o dj.

Signed.

495 BOWEN, ELIZABETH. *The Death of the Heart.* New York: Vintage K-21, 1955 (New York, 1939). 342 pp. Pap.

496 ———. *The House in Paris.* New York: Vintage K-48, 1957 (New York, 1936). 245 pp. Pap.

497 ———. *Stories by Elizabeth Bowen.* New York: Vintage K-79, 1959 [New York, 1941]. 305 + x pp. Pap.

498 CERVANTES SAAVEDRA, MIGUEL DE. *The Adventures of Don Quixote.* Trans. J. M. Cohen. Penguin Classics L10. Harmondsworth, England: Penguin, 1954 (1950). 940 pp. Pap. With dj.

499 CHEKHOV, ANTON. *Great Stories by Chekhov.* Ed., with an introduction, by David H. Greene. Trans. Constance Garnett. Sunrise Semester Library. New York: Dell Publishing, Laurel LC126, 1959. 256 pp. Pap.

500 ————. *Selected Stories*. Introduction by Lucy M. Cores. Classics Club. New York: Walter J. Black, [1943] [New York, 1929]. 320 + xvii pp.

501 CHENEY, BRAINARD. *This Is Adam*. New York: McDowell, Obolensky, [1958]. 294 pp.
    Signed. Marginal lining, p. 180.

502 CLAYTON, JOHN BELL. *The Strangers Were There: Selected Stories*. New York: Macmillan, 1957. 214 + viii pp.

503 COLETTE, SIDONIE GABRIELLE CLAUDINE. *My Mother's House* [*La Maison de Claudine*]. Trans. Una Vicenzo Troubridge and Enid McLeod. *The Vagabond* [*La Vagabonde*]. Trans. Enid McLeod. Garden City, N.Y.: Doubleday, Anchor A62, 1955 (New York, 1953; 1955) (1923; 1910). 311 pp. Pap.

504 COMPTON-BURNETT, IVY. *Brothers and Sisters*. New York: Zero Press, 1956. 273 pp.

505 ————. *A Heritage and Its History*. New York: Simon and Schuster, 1960. 249 pp.

506 CONRAD, JOSEPH. *Almayer's Folly: A Story of an Eastern River*. New York: Penguin 619, 1947 [New York, 1895]. 155 pp. Pap.

507 ————. *Lord Jim*. Introduction by J. Donald Adams. New York: Modern Library 186, [1931] [New York, 1921]. 417 + ix pp.
    Signed. Marginal linings on pp. 141–42, 177, 214.
    "Indeed his torpid demeanour concealed nothing: it had that mysterious, almost miraculous, power of producing striking effects by means impossible of detection which is the last word of the highest art" (marginal lining, pp. 141–42).
    "There were his fine sensibilities, his fine feelings, his fine longings—a sort of sublimated, idealized selfishness. He was—if you allow me to say so—very fine; very fine—and very unfortunate" (marginal lining, p. 177).
    "A man that is born falls into a dream like a man who falls into the sea. If he tries to climb out into the air as inexperienced people endeavour to do, he drowns—*nicht wahr?* . . .

No! I tell you! The way is to the destructive element submit yourself, and with the exertions of your hands and feet in the water make the deep, deep sea keep you up. So if you ask me—how to be?" (marginal lining, p. 214).

508 ———. *Nostromo.* Introduction by Robert Penn Warren. New York: Modern Library 275, 1951 [New York, 1904]. [631] + xliii pp.

Marginal linings on pp. xxvi, xxxvii, 45. Underlinings on pp. xix, xxxvii, xxxviii. Marginalia: "?" p. xxix; "see meaning / see mystery / contemplation next," p. xxxvii.

"We must sometimes force ourselves to remember that the act of creation is not simply a projection of temperament, but a criticism and purging of temperament" (part of marginal lining, p. xxvi).

"But every subject in the region of intellect and emotion must have a morality of its own if it is treated at all sincerely; and even the most artful writer will give himself (and his morality) away in about every third sentence" (encircled, p. xxxvii; quoting Conrad).

". . . that asceticism of sentiment" (complete underlining, p. xxxviii).

509 ———. Copy 2.

510 ———. *The Portable Conrad.* Ed., with an introduction and notes, by Morton Dauwen Zabel. New York: Viking Press, Viking Portable Library 33, 1947. 760 + vi pp.

Letters, p. 578.

511 ———. *The Rescue: A Romance of the Shallows.* Garden City, N.Y.: Doubleday, Anchor A199, 1960 [New York, 1920]. 387 + x pp. Pap.

512 ———. *The Secret Agent: A Simple Tale.* Garden City, N.Y.: Doubleday, Anchor A8, 1953 [New York, 1907]. 253 pp. Pap.

Letters, p. 63.

513 ———. *Under Western Eyes.* Introduction by Morton Dauwen Zabel. New Classics Series NC33. New York:

James Laughlin, New Directions, 1951 [New York 1910, 1911]. 382 + xxxvi pp.

Signed "F. O'Connor 1954."

Letters, p. 63.

514 ———. *Victory*. New York: Modern Library 34, [1921] [New York, 1915]. 385 + xvi pp.

Signed, dated 1952.

515 ———. *Youth and Two Other Stories* (*Heart of Darkness* and *The End of the Tether*). New York: McClure, Phillips, 1905 (New York, 1903). 381 pp. W/o dj.

516 CRANE, STEPHEN. *Stephen Crane: Stories and Tales*. Ed., with an introduction, by Robert Wooster Stallman. New York: Vintage K-10, 1958 (New York, 1955). 350 + xxxii pp.

517 CUMMINGS, E. E. *The Enormous Room*. Introduction by Cummings. New York: Modern Library 214, [1934] [New York, 1922]. 332 + xviii pp.

Signed, dated July 1952. O'Connor has checked these titles on the dj: Aquinas, *Introduction to St. Thomas Aquinas;* Balzac, *Père Goriot* and *Eugénie Grandet;* Chaucer, *The Canterbury Tales;* Conrad, *Nostromo;* Hawthorne, *The Scarlet Letter;* Melville, *Moby Dick.*

518 DICKENS, CHARLES. *Great Expectations*. Introduction by Edward Wagenknecht. New York: Pocket Library PL50, 1956. 466 + xi pp. Pap.

519 ———. *Hard Times: For These Times*. Introduction by William W. Watt. New York: Holt, Rinehart and Winston, Rinehart Editions 95, 1960 [New York, 1958]. 274 + xliii pp. Pap.

520 ———. *Oliver Twist*. Introduction by Graham Greene. Novel Library 35. London: Hamish Hamilton, 1950 (London, 1838). 511 + xx pp.

521 [BLIXEN, KAREN.] DINESON, ISAK. *Seven Gothic Tales*. Introduction by Dorothy Canfield. New York: Modern Library 54, [1934]. 420 + x pp. W/o dj.

Signed.

Letters, p. 253.

522 DOSTOEVSKY, FYODOR. *The Best Short Stories of Dostoevsky.*
Trans., with an introduction, by David Magarshack. New
York: Modern Library 293, [1955]. 322 + xxiii pp.

523 ———. *Crime and Punishment.* Trans. Constance Garnett.
Ed. Carl Van Doren. Introduction by Alfred Kazin. Illus-
trated by Ruth Gikow. Living Library. Cleveland: World
Publishing, 1947. 499 pp. Illus. W/o dj.
   Signed.

524 ———. *The Devils (The Possessed).* Trans., with an introduction, by David Magarshack. Harmondsworth, England:
Penguin Classics L35, n.d. (1953). 669 + xvii pp. Pap. With
dj.

525 DURRELL, LAWRENCE. *Justine.* New York: E. P. Dutton,
[1957]. 253 pp.

526 [EVANS, MARY ANNE.] ELIOT, GEORGE. *The Best-Known Novels of George Eliot.* New York: Modern Library G51, [1940].
1,350 pp.
   Texts of *Adam Bede, The Mill on the Floss, Silas Marner,* and
   Romola.

527 ———. *Middlemarch.* London: Zodiac Press, 1950 (1872). 795
pp.
   Plastic wrap labeled Grove Press, New York.
   Signed, dated 1954.

528 FAULKNER, WILLIAM. *Absalom, Absalom!* Introduction by
Harvey Breit. New York: Modern Library 271, 1951 [1936].
378 + xii pp. Map, chronology, genealogy.

529 ———. *The Mansion.* New York: Random House, [1959]. 436
pp.

530 ———. *Pylon.* New York: New American Library, Signet
863, 1951 (New York, 1935). 189 pp. Pap.

531 ———. *Sanctuary* and *Requiem for a Nun.* New York: New
American Library, Signet S1079, 1954 (New York, 1931;
1951). 336 pp. Pap.
   Letters, p. 16.

532 ———. *Three Famous Short Novels: Spotted Horses, Old Man,*

The Bear. New York: Modern Library P36, [1958]. 316 pp. Pap.

533 ———. *The Unvanquished*. New York: New American Library, Signet 977, 1952 [New York, 1938]. 160 pp. Pap.

534 FIELDING, HENRY. *The Adventures of Joseph Andrews*. Introduction by Bruce McCullough. Modern Student's Library. New York: Charles Scribner's Sons, [1930]. 402 + xlix pp. W/o dj.

535 ———. *The History of Tom Jones, a Foundling*. New York: Modern Library 185, [1940]. [886] + xxiv pp.

536 FORD, FORD MADOX. *The Good Soldier: A Tale of Passion*. Introduction by Mark Schorer. New York: Alfred A. Knopf, 1951 [1927]. 256 + xxii pp. W/o dj.

Signed, dated 1954. Bracket and check mark on p. 125.

"It was a thing like a knife that looked out of her eyes and that spoke with her voice, just now and then. It positively frightened me. I suppose that I was almost afraid to be in a world where there could be so fine a standard" (bracket and check mark, p. 125).

Letters, pp. 446–47, 469.

537 FORSTER, E. M. *A Passage to India*. New York: Modern Library 218, [1924]. 322 pp.

Signed. Marginal linings on pp. 19, 56, 86, 208, 211, 245, 264. Circled word, p. 8. Underlining, p. 8. Check mark, p. 46. Marginalia: "what a contrast," p. 7; "environs outskirts," p. 8; "Are they hardened in their resentment," p. 9; "lovingly," p. 9; "ah: zeez," p. 9; "what class of Indians?" p. 9; "occupation," p. 9; "cast off," p. 38; "summary of C.S. [?]," p. 50; "artificial," p. 87.

Letters, p. 445.

538 GOGOL, NIKOLAI. *Dead Souls*. Trans. Andrew R. MacAndrew. Foreword by Frank O'Connor. New York: New American Library, Signet CP66, 1961. 278 + xii pp. Pap.

Letters, p. 44.

539 ———. *Mirgorod*. Trans., with an introduction, by David

Magarshack. New York: Farrar, Straus and Cudahy, 1962. 275 + xi pp.

Letters, p. 498.

540 ———. *Taras Bulba: A Historical Novel of Russia and Poland.* Trans., with a preface, by Jeremiah Curtin. New York: John B. Alden, 1888. 208 + xxv pp. W/o dj.

541 GORDON, CAROLINE. *The Malefactors.* New York: Harcourt, Brace, [1956]. 312 pp.

Bulletin, 3.31.56; *Reviews*, pp. 15–16; *Letters*, pp. 129, 135, 140, 144, 145, 149, 151, 155, 157–60, 166, 169, 218, 235, 257, 273, 301, 332.

542 ———. *Old Red and Other Stories.* New York: Charles Scribner's Sons, [1963]. 256 pp.

Letters, pp. 187, 188, 200.

543 HAWKES, JOHN. *The Beetle Leg.* New York: James Laughlin, New Directions, 1951. 159 pp. W/o dj.

544 ———. *The Cannibal.* Introduction by Albert J. Guerard. New York: James Laughlin, Direction 13, 1949. 223 + xiv pp.

545 HAWTHORNE, NATHANIEL. *Collected Works.* Masterworks Library. New York: Greystone Press, n.d. 502 + vii pp.

Includes *The Scarlet Letter, The House of the Seven Gables,* and "the best of the" *Twice-Told Tales.*

Letters, pp. 70, 457.

546 ———. *The House of the Seven Gables.* New York: Pocket 52, 1951 [New York, 1940]. 370 + viii pp. Pap.

547 ———. *The Marble Faun, or The Romance of Monte Beni.* Introduction by Maxwell Geismar. New York: Pocket Library PL59, 1958. 388 + xii pp. Pap.

548 ———. *The Scarlet Letter: A Romance.* Introduction by John C. Gerber. New York: Modern Library 93, [1950]. 300 + xxxiv pp.

549 HUGHES, RICHARD. *A High Wind in Jamaica* (*The Innocent Voyage*). Introduction by Isabel Peterson. New York: Modern Library 112, [1932], [1929]. 399 + xxii + ix pp. W/o dj. Illus.

Letters, pp. 441, 480.

550 JAMES, HENRY. *The Portrait of a Lady.* New York: Modern Library 107, n.d., [1881]. [438] pp.

Letters, p. 226.

551 ———. *What Maisie Knew.* Garden City, N.Y.: Doubleday, Anchor A43, 1954 (1897, 1908). 280 pp. Pap.

Includes James's Preface for the New York edition.

Letters, pp. 332–33.

552 JONES, MADISON. *A Buried Land.* New York: Viking Press, 1963. 295 pp.

Half-title page signed "For Flannery, With all respects, Madison."

Letters, p. 529.

553 ———. *Forest of the Night.* New York: Harcourt, Brace, [1960]. 305 pp.

Check mark on p. 204.

Letters, pp. 348, 372.

554 ———. *The Innocent.* New York: Harcourt, Brace, [1957]. 370 pp.

Letters, pp. 206, 211, 240–41.

555 JOYCE, JAMES. *Dubliners.* Introduction by Padraic Colum. New York: Modern Library 124, [1926]. 288 + xiii pp. W/o dj.

Signed. Marginal linings on pp. 7, 12, 13. Underlinings on pp. 7, 10, 11, 12, 14, 15. Marginalia: "the mysterious strong words," p. 10; "1 Your huntin' something she drawled You lost something Something on your mind," "2 Mrs [?] eyed with only a slight wink," "[?] that's alright, sugar," inside back flyleaf. Marked in catalog at end: Henry Adams, *The Education of Henry Adams;* Ambrose Bierce, *In the Midst of Life;* Isak Dinesen, *Seven Gothic Tales;* Fyodor Dostoyevsky, *Crime and Punishment;* Gustave Flaubert, *Madame Bovary;* André Gide, *The Counterfeiters;* Ellen Glasgow, *Barren Ground; Great German Short Novels and Stories;* Anthony Trollope, *Barchester Towers* and *The Warden.*

Letters, pp. 84, 130, 203, 379.

556 KAFKA, FRANZ. *Selected Short Stories of Franz Kafka.* Trans. Willa Muir and Edwin Muir. Introduction by Philip Rahv. New York: Modern Library 283, 1952 [Prague, 1936, 1937]. 328 + xxii pp.

Signed, dated 1952.

557 LAFAYETTE, MADAME MADELEINE DE. *The Princess of Cleves* (*La Princesse de Clèves*). Trans., with an introduction, by Nancy Mitford. New Classics Series NC31. New York: James Laughlin, [1951]. 210 + xxviii pp.

558 LANDA, MICHEL. *The Cactus Grove.* Trans. Edward Hyams. London: Longmans Green, 1960; *Les Cloches de Plomb* [Paris, 1959]. 206 pp.

559 LARDNER, RING. *The Collected Short Stories of Ring Lardner.* New York: Modern Library 211, n.d. [1929]. 467 + viii pp.

Signed, dated 1953. O'Connor has marked "The Golden Honeymoon," pp. 221–35, and "A Caddy's Diary," pp. 393–407, in table of contents, p. viii. Original title: *Round Up.*

560 LESKOV, NIKOLAÏ. *Selected Tales.* Trans. David Magarshack. Introduction by V. S. Pritchett. New York: Farrar, Straus and Cudahy, 1961. 300 + xviii pp.

561 LEWIS, WYNDHAM. *The Red Priest.* London: Methuen, 1956. 298 + vi pp.

Signed, dated 1957.

Letters, p. 217.

562 ———. *The Revenge for Love.* Chicago: Henry Regnery, 1952. 341 pp.

Signed, dated 1953.

563 ———. *Self Condemned.* London: Methuen, 1954. 407 + vi pp.

Letters, pp. 174, 179–80.

564 MALAMUD, BERNARD. *The Magic Barrel.* New York: Farrar, Straus and Cudahy, 1958. 214 pp.

Signed, dated 1958.

Letters, pp. 287, 288, 310.

565 Mann, Thomas. *Death in Venice and Seven Other Stories.*
Trans. H. T. Lowe-Porter. New York: Vintage K-3, 1954
(New York, 1930). 404 pp. Pap.

566 Mansfield, Katherine. *The Garden Party.* New York: Modern Library 129, n.d. [New York, 1922]. 255 pp.

567 Manzoni, Alessandro. *The Betrothed (I Promessi Sposi): A Tale of Seventeenth Century Milan.* Trans., with a preface, by Archibald Colquhoun. Everyman's Library 999. London: J. M. Dent and Sons, 1959 (London, 1951). [536] + xxvi pp.
"Christmas 1961 To Flannery with a promise of prayers. Father Dodwell" on flyleaf.
Letters, p. 297.

568 Mauriac, François. *Flesh and Blood (La Chair et Le Sang).* Trans. Gerard Hopkins. New York: Farrar, Straus, 1955. 190 pp.
Letters, pp. 98, 130, 231, 570.

569 ———. *The Frontenacs (La Mystère Frontenac).* Trans. Gerard Hopkins. New York: Farrar, Straus and Cudahy, 1961. 185 pp.

570 ———. *The Lamb (L'Agneau).* Trans. Gerard Hopkins. New York: Farrar, Straus and Cudahy, 1955. 156 pp.
Letters, p. 241.

571 ———. *Lines of Life (Destins).* Trans. Gerard Hopkins. New York: Farrar, Straus and Cudahy, [1957]. 153 pp.
Bulletin, 10.26.57; *Reviews,* pp. 44–45; *Letters,* pp. 237, 241.

572 ———. *The Loved and the Unloved.* Trans. Gerard Hopkins. Postscript by Mauriac. New York: Pellegrini and Cudahy, 1952. 153 pp.

573 ———. *Questions of Precedence (Préséances).* Trans. Gerard Hopkins. New York: Farrar, Straus and Cudahy, 1959 (1921). 158 pp.
Letters, p. 345.

574 ———. *Thérèse: A Portrait in Four Parts.* Trans. Gerard Hopkins. Foreword by Mauriac. New York: Henry Holt, 1947. 383 pp.

575 ———. *The Unknown Sea.* Trans. Gerard Hopkins. New York: Henry Holt, 1948. 236 pp.

576 ———. *Vipers' Tangle.* Trans. Warre B. Wells. Garden City, N.Y.: Doubleday, Image D51, 1957. 199 pp. Pap.

577 ———. *The Weakling (Le Sagouin)* and *The Enemy (Le Mal).* Trans. Gerard Hopkins. New York: Pellegrini and Cudahy, [1952] (1951, 1935 respectively). 219 pp.

578 MAXWELL, WILLIAM. *The Folded Leaf.* New York: Vintage K78, 1959 (New York, 1945). 274 pp. Pap.

579 MELVILLE, HERMAN. *Moby Dick: or, The White Whale.* Boston: L. C. Page, 1950. 533 + xii pp.
    Letters, p. 56.

580 MEREDITH, GEORGE. *Diana of the Crossways.* Introduction by Arthur Symons. New York: Modern Library 14, n.d. 447 + xvi pp. W/o dj.

581 NABOKOV, VLADIMIR. *The Real Life of Sebastian Knight.* Introduction by Conrad Brenner. Norfolk, Conn.: New Directions, [1959] [1941]. 205 + [xvi] pp.
    Letters, pp. 339–40, 343.

582 NIN, ANAÏS. *Seduction of the Minotaur.* London: Peter Owen, [1961]. 159 pp.
    "Dean Owens" on flyleaf.

583 O'CONNOR, FRANK. *Stories by Frank O'Connor.* Foreword by Frank O'Connor. New York: Vintage K-29, [1956]. 275 + viii pp. Pap.

584 O'FLAHERTY, LIAM. *The Stories of Liam O'Flaherty.* Introduction by Vivian Mercier. New York: Devin-Adair, 1956. 419 + x pp.

585 PORTER, KATHERINE ANNE. *Flowering Judas and Other Stories.* New introduction by Porter. New York: Modern Library 88, [1953]. 285 pp. W/o dj.
    O'Connor has checked the following from the catalog in the book: Henry Adams, *The Education of Henry Adams;* Sherwood Anderson, *Winesburg, Ohio;* Edward Bellamy, *Looking Backward;* Arnold Bennett, *The Old Wives' Tale;* Henri

Bergson, *Creative Evolution;* Ambrose Bierce, *In the Midst of Life;* Erskine Caldwell, *God's Little Acre;* Joseph Conrad, *Lord Jim;* Daniel Defoe, *Moll Flanders;* Isak Dinesen, *Seven Gothic Tales;* Fyodor Dostoyevsky, *Crime and Punishment* and *The Brothers Karamazov;* William Faulkner, *Sanctuary;* Henry Fielding, *Tom Jones;* Gustave Flaubert, *Madame Bovary;* E. M. Forster, *A Passage to India;* André Gide, *The Counterfeiters;* Ellen Glasgow, *Barren Ground;* Thomas Hardy, *Jude the Obscure, The Return of the Native,* and *Tess of the D'Urbervilles;* Ernest Hemingway, *A Farewell to Arms;* Henry James, *The Portrait of a Lady;* James Joyce, *Dubliners;* W. Somerset Maugham, *Of Human Bondage;* André Maurois, *Disraeli;* George Meredith, *Diana of the Crossways;* Miscellaneous, *An Anthology of Light Verse, Best Russian Short Stories, including Bunin's "The Gentleman from San Francisco,"* and *Great Modern Short Stories;* Walter Pater, *Marius the Epicurean;* Katherine Anne Porter, *Flowering Judas;* Schopenhauer, *The Philosophy of Schopenhauer;* Tobias Smollett, *Humphrey Clinker;* John Steinbeck, *In Dubious Battle;* Stendhal, *The Red and the Black;* Laurence Sterne, *Tristram Shandy;* Lytton Strachey, *Eminent Victorians;* William Thackeray, *Henry Esmond;* Leo Tolstoy, *Anna Karenina;* Edith Wharton, *The Age of Innocence;* Virginia Woolf, *Mrs. Dalloway* and *To the Lighthouse.*

Letters, p. 98.

586 ———. *The Old Order: Stories of the South*. Harcourt, Brace, Harvest HB6, n.d. 182 pp. Pap.

Includes portions of *Flowering Judas; Pale Horse, Pale Rider;* and *The Leaning Tower.*

587 ———. *Pale Horse, Pale Rider: Three Short Novels*. New York: Modern Library 45, [1939]. 264 pp.

Contents: *Old Mortality, Noon Wine,* and *Pale Horse, Pale Rider.*

Letters, p. 485.

588 POWERS, J. F. *Morte D'Urban*. Garden City, N.Y.: Doubleday, 1962. 336 pp.

Southern Cross, 11.27.65; *Catholic Week*, 11.29.63, p. 7; *Reviews*, pp. 167–68; *Letters*, pp. 496, 505, 511, 570.

589 PURDY, JAMES. *Color of Darkness: Eleven Stories and a Novella.* New York: James Laughlin, New Directions, [1957]. 175 pp.
Letters, pp. 264, 291, 292–93.

590 RICHARDSON, SAMUEL. *Clarissa: Or, the History of a Young Lady.* Ed., with an introduction, by John Angus Burrell. Abridged text. New York: Modern Library 10, [1950]. 786 + xiv pp.

591 ROEHLER, KLAUS. *The Dignity of Night: Seven Stories.* Trans. John and Necke Mander. Philadelphia: J. B. Lippincott, Keystone KB 27, 1961; *Die Würde der Nacht* [Munich, 1958]. 128 pp. Pap.

592 RUBIN, LOUIS. *The Golden Weather.* New York: Atheneum, 1961. 303 pp.
"For Flannery O'Connor—much the better builder—L. Rubin 4/3/63" written on title page.

593 SANTOS, BIENVENIDO N. *Brother, My Brother: A Collection of Stories.* Introduction by Leonard Casper. Manila: Benipayo, 1960. 244 + xiii pp. In English.
Signed.

594 SCHNABEL, ERNST. *The Voyage Home (Der Sechste Gesang).* Trans. Denver Lindley. New York: Harcourt, Brace, [1958]. 184 pp.

595 SINGER, ISAAC BASHEVIS. *The Spinoza of Market Street.* Trans. Martha Glicklich, Cecil Hemley, Shulamith Charney, Elizabeth Pollet, Mirra Ginsburg, Joel Blocker, Gertrude Hirschler, Elaine Gottlieb, and June Ruth Flaum. New York: Farrar, Straus and Cudahy, 1961. 214 pp.
Letters, p. 473.

596 SPARK, MURIEL. *The Ballad of Peckham Rye.* Philadelphia: J. B. Lippincott, [1960]. 160 pp.
"Retreat House Library, Lake Dallas, Texas" stamped on flyleaf.

597 ———. *The Girls of Slender Means*. London: Macmillan, 1963. [183] pp.

    Letters, p. 577.

598 SWIFT, JONATHAN. *Gulliver's Travels: An Account of the Four Voyages into Several Remote Regions of the World*. Introduction by Jacques Barzun. Illustrations by Luis Quintanilla. New York: Crown, 1947. 358 + xxvi pp. Illus.

599 TAYLOR, PETER. *Happy Families Are All Alike: A Collection of Stories*. New York: McDowell, Obolensky, [1959]. 305 pp.

    Signed, dated 1960.

600 ———. *A Long Fourth and Other Stories*. Introduction by Robert Penn Warren. New York: Harcourt, Brace, [1948]. 166 + x pp. W/o dj.

    Signed.

    Letters, p. 121.

601 THACKERAY, WILLIAM MAKEPEACE. *Vanity Fair: A Novel without a Hero*. Introduction by John Marquand. Drawings by Robert Ball. New York: Random House, [1958]. 543 + xvii pp. W/o dj.

602 TOLSTOY, COUNT LEO. *Anna Karenina*. Trans. Constance Garnett. Introduction by Henri Troyat, trans. J. Robert Loy. New York: Modern Library 37, [1950]. 950 + xviii pp.

603 ———. *The Death of Ivan Ilych and Other Stories*. Afterword by David Magarshack. *The Death of Ivan Ilych*, *The Kreutzer Sonata*, and *Master and Man* trans. Aylmer Maude. *Family Happiness* trans. J. D. Duff. New York: New American Library, Signet CD13, 1960. 304 pp. Pap.

    Marginalia: "Cedar 3–3568 Cleo," p. 100; "La 3–7211 Louis," p. 101.

604 ———. *War and Peace*. Trans. Constance Garnett. New York: Modern Library G1, [1931]. 1,136 pp. W/o dj.

605 TROLLOPE, ANTHONY. *Barchester Towers* and *The Warden*. Introduction by Harlan Hatcher. New York: Modern Library 41, [1950]. 746 + xx pp.

606 TURGENEV, IVAN S. *Fathers and Sons.* Trans. Constance Garnett. Rev. and ed., with an introduction, by Lucy M. Cores. Classics Club. New York: Walter J. Black, [1942]. 345 + xxvii pp.

Signed "M. F. O'Connor 1944."

607 ———. *A Sportsman's Notebook.* Trans. Charles and Natasha Hepburn. New York: Viking Press, Compass C-24, 1957 (1950). [398] + [vii] pp.

608 UPDIKE, JOHN. *The Same Door: Short Stories.* New York: Alfred A. Knopf, 1959. [242] pp.

Signed.

Letters, pp. 339, 340.

609 WAUGH, EVELYN. *Men at Arms* and *Officers and Gentlemen.* New York: Dell Publishing, Laurel LX136, 1961 [1952 and 1955, respectively]. 512 pp. Pap.

Letters, p. 522.

610 ———. *Vile Bodies* and *Black Mischief.* New York: Dell Publishing, Laurel LX122, 1960 [1930 and 1932, respectively]. 381 pp. Pap.

Signed on front cover.

611 WELTY, EUDORA. *The Bride of the Innisfallen and Other Stories.* New York: Harcourt, Brace, [1955]. 207 pp.

Signed, dated 1955.

612 WEST, NATHANAEL. *The Day of the Locust.* Introduction by Richard B. Gehman. New Classics NC29. New York: James Laughlin, [1950]. 167 + xxiii pp.

Letters, p. 16.

613 WHARTON, EDITH. *The Age of Innocence.* New York: Modern Library 229, n.d. [New York, 1920]. [365] pp.

614 WISEMAN, NICHOLAS, CARDINAL. *Fabiloa: Or, The Church of the Catacombs.* London: Burns, Oates and Washbourne, 1922. 324 + x pp. W/o dj. Partly unbound.

"For Sister Mary Alice July 1962 Dupont Wright" written on flyleaf. "Dupont Wright Goggins, Ga." stamped on inside front cover.

615 WOOLF, VIRGINIA. *Jacob's Room* and *The Waves*. New York: Harcourt, Brace, Harvest HB 7 [1959] [1923 and 1931, respectively]. 383 pp. Pap.

616 ———. *Mrs. Dalloway*. Introduction by Virginia Woolf. New York: Modern Library 96, [1928] [New York, 1925]. 296 + ix pp. W/o dj.

Signed, dated 1947.

617 YOURCENAR, MARGUERITE. *Hadrian's Memoirs* (*Mémoires d'Hadrien*). Trans. Grace Frick in collaboration with Yourcenar. With note by Yourcenar. Garden City, N.Y.: Doubleday, Anchor A108, 1957 [1951; New York, 1954]. 309 pp. Pap.

"George Haslam New York, N.Y. April *1960*" on inside front cover.

Journals and Magazines

618 *The Abbey Message*. Ed. Rev. Gabriel Franks, O.S.B., 23 (3) (December 1962).

O'Connor is used as opening example in Jerome Knoedel, O.S.B., "Bible Reading: Practical Problems Aplenty," p. 6.

619 *Accent*. Ed. Kerker Quinn et al., 6 (4) (Summer 1946).

Includes "The Geranium," pp. 245–53. Reprint of story enclosed with following corrections: "er" changed to "of," p. 245, line 7; "er" changed to "have," p. 245, line 25; "like" changed to "liked," p. 246, 6 lines from bottom; "Dudley would grin" blacked out, p. 247, line 1; single quotation mark changed to double quotation mark, p. 248, line 11; "er" corrected to "of," p. 249, line 17; "this" corrected to "his," p. 249, line 33; "kind er" crossed out, p. 250, line 22; "He felt heavy in his stomach" crossed out, p. 250, line 27; "thout even the hens knowing it" changed to "without" and then all six words crossed out, p. 250, line 34; "him" changed to "he," p. 250, line 36; "was" corrected to "were," p. 250, line 36; "em" changed to "them," p. 250, line 37; "quickern" changed to "quicker then," p. 250, line 38; "er" changed to "have," p. 251, line 8; "er" changed to "have," "er" to "of," "er" to "have," and "em" to "them," all p. 251, line 14; "er" changed to "have," "em" changed to "them," p. 251, line 16; "till" changed to "until," p. 252, line 1.

620 *America.* Ed. Thurston N. Davis. 108 (26) (June 29, 1963).

Notes and markings by Janet McKane as follows: table of contents: check marks, p. 892.

For John LaFarge, "Church Leaders Stand Up to Be Counted": marginal linings, p. 897; marginalia: "Atlanta," p. 897.

For editorial on "Varieties of Stupidity": marginal linings, p. 899; underlinings, p. 899; marginalia: "discernment perception judgement," p. 899.

For Bernard J. Coughlin, S.J., "Interfaith Dialogue and Church-State Issues": marginal linings, pp. 901, 902; underlinings, pp. 901, 902; asterisk, p. 902; marginalia: "Jewish view," p. 901; "start-There is a militant, determined, realistic effort in the field of education to devaluate/remove Christian symbols and thought from all areas of the curriculum & textbooks and to insert Jewish areas of thought. This is very frequent—at the expense of degrading, satirizing Christian Religion or equating it only with secular symbols—as Santa Claus or Bunny, & pagan traditions—It all tends toward sensitive misunderstandings/a definite cleavage," p. 902.

621 ———. 109 (22) (November 30, 1963).

Notes and markings by Janet McKane as follows: Cover: "Flannery—good articles on many areas of pertinent interest./Janet"; "pg 707—Mystery and Life" next to essay on Gabriel Marcel; "good—pg 711" next to essay on secular campus.

Table of contents: check marks, p. 690.

Correspondence on "The Deputy": circled and checked, p. 691.

For editorial on "The Jews and Vatican II": marginal lining, p. 698; brackets, p. 698; check mark at title, p. 698; asterisk, p. 698. "Church Aid, Church Unity": asterisk at title, p. 700.

For Donald R. Campion and Daniel J. O'Hanlon, "Council Jottings: Dream Fulfilled," marginal lining, p. 701; for "Side Drama," marginal linings, p. 701; for "Ecumenism's Impact," marginal linings, p. 701; check marks, pp. 701, 702; asterisk, p. 701.

For John Courtney Murray, S.J., "On Religious Liberty," marginal linings, p. 705; brackets, p. 704; numbers in margin, pp. 704, 706.

For Michael Moffitt, "Gabriel Marcel at Gonzaga": marginal linings, pp. 707, 708, 709; brackets, pp. 707, 708, 709; underlinings, pp. 707, 708, 709; asterisk, p. 709; marginalia: "Theme = how can man recapture a sense of the 'sacredness of life' in this modern age of pragmatic technology?" p. 708; "Theme," p. 708; "—He felt his hunger no longer as a pain but as a tide. He felt it rising in himself through time and darkness rising through the centuries [?Tavard]," p. 709.

For Charles Davis, "Theological Asides": marginal linings, p. 710; underlining, p. 710; check marks, p. 710; numbers in margin, p. 710; marginalia: "T de C.," p. 710.

For "Crisis in the Colleges," book review of Richard Butler, O.P., *God on the Secular Campus:* marginal linings, pp. 711, 712; brackets, p. 711; underlining, p. 711; check mark, p. 711; asterisks, pp. 711, 712; marginalia: "Newman = to combat modern secularism 1) sense of God's presence 2) a good life 2) knowledge-deep and embracing & ability to articulate," p. 711.

622 *The American Benedictine Review.* Ed. Colman J. Barry, O.S.B. 14 (2) (June 1963).

623 *The American Scholar.* Ed. Hiram Haydn. 29 (3) (Summer 1960).

With poem "Sunday at the Peacock Cage" by Edward Kessler, pp. 386–87; line of poem checked reads: "Or those blankets undertakers spread over graves." Letter enclosed, dated September 18, 1961: "Dear Miss O'Connor—A steady fan of your writing, I am even more devoted to you after learning of your devotion to peacocks. Here's a copy of *The American Scholar*, which contains my few words on the bird. With admiration, Edward Kessler, English Department, Rutgers University, New Brunswick, New Jersey."

624 *Bulletin of Wesleyan College, Ga.* 41 (1) (January 1961).

Foreword by Norman Charles.

"Recent Southern Fiction: A Panel Discussion"; panel included Katherine Anne Porter, Caroline Gordon, Madison Jones, and Flannery O'Connor; Louis D. Rubin, Jr., was moderator.

625 ———. Copy 2.

626 *Catholic Mind.* Ed. Thurston N. Davis, S.J. 60 (1,160) (February 1962).

S. Z. Young's "Theology and Population" circled on cover. Includes O'Connor's "The Mystery of Suffering," adapted from *A Memoir of Mary Ann*, reprinted in *Mystery and Manners*, 213–28, pp. 22–29.

Letters, p. 468.

627 ———. Copy 2.

628 *The Critic.* Ed. Paul K. Cuneo. 19 (4) (February-March 1961).

Includes O'Connor's "The Partridge Festival," pp. 20–23, 82–85.

629 *Critique: Studies in Modern Fiction.* Ed. Allan Hanna et al. 4 (3) (Winter 1961–62).

Special issue on Wright Morris.

630 *Cross and Crown.* Ed. John J. McDonald, O.P. 16 (1) (March 1964).

Annotations by Janet McKane: for Barbara Dent, "Entombment and Resurrection": marginal linings, pp. 31, 32, 34, 37, 102; brackets, p. 22; underlining, p. 32; check mark, p. 26; marginalia: "B. Dent," p. 33.

For review of Hans Joachim Schoeps, *The Jewish-Christian Argument:* marginal lining, p. 102.

631 ———. 16 (2) (June 1964).

Notes by Janet McKane on cover concerning Hawthorne essay, pp. 142–65, and review of Karl Rahner, *The Church and the Sacraments,* pp. 222–24. Check mark, p. 222.

For Sr. Theresa Margaret, O.D.C., "The Otherness of God": marginal lining, p. 179; brackets, p. 179.

"One of the impoverishments of this age is that we have lost our sense of awe, even on the material plane" (bracket, p. 179).

632 *Cross Currents.* Ed. Joseph L. Caulfield et al. 4 (4) (Fall 1954).

For A. J. Maydieu, "Christians at Work": marginal lining, p. 303; underlining, p. 303.

633 ———. 5 (1) (Winter 1955).

Poulet, *Studies in Human Time* (see entry 425), chap. 1, pp. 51–75; review of Guardini, *The Lord* (see entry 128), p. 96.

For Walter Dirks, "How Can I Know What God Wants of Me?": marginal lining, p. 85.

"It was not a pious glance, but a medical observation that the Good Samaritan gave the man who was bleeding from his wounds. Situations engage man in many secular matters and give him a variety of choices. That is why the reflections of situation-ethics can often appear quite profane. As they are concerned with the man who is present, and take his corporal, psychical, and intellectual totality seriously, they often place material needs in bold relief, and this situational imagination sometimes discovers needs which are quite different from those generally conceded and presented as standard. The spiritual reality which the Christian recognizes even in apparently profane reality is fraternity, not as a spontaneous feeling (don't blood brothers often behave with more dryness towards one another than friends or lovers?) but as an elementary reality which Christ has not only proclaimed, but realized, and which is realizable in him and with him. This reality leaves to the secular order its own density; it does not have recourse to pious phrases in order to calm someone's hunger, but gives him something to eat. Or it may even give the child a useful slap" (marginal lining, p. 85).

634 ———. 5 (4) (Fall 1955).

Front cover signed. Review of Von Hügel, *Letters from Baron Friedrich von Hügel to a Niece* (see entry 46), pp. 374–75.

For Maurice S. Friedman, "Healing Through Meeting: Martin Buber and Psychotherapy": marginal linings, pp. 299, 304, 305; underlinings, pp. 299, 301; marginalia: "fiction," p. 301; "fiction," p. 304; "fiction," p. 305.

". . . but of a concrete imagining of the other side which does not at the same time lose sight of one's own" (underlining, marked "fiction," p. 301).

"Such surprise-response will, of course, never emerge when the analyst approaches unconscious material theoretically. He will then see only what he expects to see and neglect, distort, or overlook what does not fit his scheme" (marginal lining, marked "Fiction," quoting Theodor Reik, p. 304).

". . . a trying 'to get *within* and to live the attitudes expressed instead of observing them' " (marginal lining, marked "fiction," quoting Carl R. Rogers, p. 305).

Letters, p. 191.

635 ———. 6 (2) (Spring 1956).

For Friedrich Heer, "The Rebirth of Catholic Obedience": marginal lining, p. 121.

636 ———. 6 (4) (Fall 1956).

For Jacques Maritain, "Freudianism and Psychoanalysis": marginal lining, pp. 308, 309, 322, 323; check marks, pp.

310, 314; correction of text, p. 313; marginalia: "Epistle to Cor. 4th Sunday Advent," p. 308.

For J. Loewenberg, "The Comedy of Immediacy in Hegel's Phenomenology": entire essay (pp. 345–58) cut out and missing.

For Romano Guardini, "Dostoyevsky's Idiot, A Symbol of Christ": marginal lining, p. 364; underlining, p. 368.

Letters, pp. 191, 243.

"The existence of Myshkin would seem to be a direct verification of this axiom: the highest values raised to their maximum, but incarnated in an existence which is incapable of affirming itself in this world" (marginal lining, p. 364).

Checked on back cover with calculation for purchasing reprints: "RIMAUD on psychologists vs. morality; MORREN on the Catholic & science; GUARDINI on myth & revelation; MARITAIN on psychoanalysis; TAURES on crisis-theology; HARPER on poetic justice; HATZFELD on Bernanos; DANIÉLOU on history; M. MORÉ on Graham Greene; DIRKS on the future of missions; CASSERLEY: depth-psychology & theology; ROCHDIEU on affective dynamics & religious sentiment."

637 ———. Copy 2.

For Peter Cardinal Gerlier, "The Co-Existence of Believers and Unbelievers": marginal lining, p. 285; underlining, p. 292; marginalia: "von Hugel's friend" (referring to Abbé Huvelin), p. 292.

For Jacques Maritain, "Freudianism and Psychoanalysis": check marks, pp. 319, 320.

"The whole of Freudian philosophy rests upon the prejudice of a radical denial of spirituality and freedom. As a result, experimental insights, which are often correct, become hardened philosophically into the worst errors" (passage marked with check mark, p. 320).

638 ———. With expanded editorial board. 9 (4) (Fall 1959).

Signed on front cover. Includes essay by Pierre Teilhard de Chardin, "Building the Earth."

639 ——————. 12 (1) (Winter 1962).

640 ——————. 12 (4) (Fall 1962).

Signed on front cover.

For Thomas Sartory, "The Council and Ecumenical Concern": marginal lining, p. 404; underlinings, pp. 400, 401; check marks, pp. 402, 404, 405; exclamation marks, p. 401; question mark, p. 404.

641 ——————. 13 (2) (Spring 1963).

John J. Harmon, "The Church in the City" underlined on front cover (with asterisk by his name) and in table of contents on inside front cover.

For Peter Fransen, "Three Ways of Dogmatic Thought": marginal lining, p. 142; underlinings, pp. 141, 142, 143.

For John J. Harmon, "The Church in the City": underlining, title, p. 150; check marks, title, p. 150, 162 (with asterisk).

For Henry G. Wolz, "The *Phaedo:* Plato and the Dramatic Approach to Philosophy": marginal lining, p. 184; marginalia: "Death," p. 184.

For "Annual Review of Philosophy 1962–63": marginal lining, p. 196 (on Heidegger and Merleau-Ponty as important new sources for existentialism and phenomenology).

For review of Kenneth Gallagher, *The Philosophy of Gabriel Marcel:* underlinings, pp. 198, 199.

For Eldon M. Talley, "The Place of the Layman": marginal lining, p. 264; underlining, p. 264; asterisk at beginning and on p. 263.

For David Burrell, "Barth: Touchstone of Catholicity": marginal lining, p. 265; asterisks, p. 264.

642 *Esprit.* Ed. Charles J. Keffer. 6 (1) (Spring 1963). A student publication of the University of Scranton.

643 ——————. Copy 2.

644 *Fresco.* Ed. William F. Dwyer and Jerome L. Mazzaro. 1 (2) (Winter 1961).

Noted on front cover: "p. 100." Includes O'Connor's "The

Novelist and Free Will," pp. 100–101, with this note: "This essay is made up of sections of two letters written by Miss O'Connor to Winifred McCarthy in response to specific questions which Miss McCarthy posed regarding the nature of free will in Miss O'Connor's books. It is printed with the permission of Miss O'Connor, because as editors we feel that it manages to clear up some of the confusion which critics have stated existed in her writing" (editor's note, p. 100).

645 ———. Copy 2.

646 *Good Housekeeping.* Ed. Wade H. Nichols. 153 (6) (December 1961).

Includes "A Memoir of Mary Ann," pp. 65–72, with introductory note only by O'Connor, p. 66.

Letters, p. 450.

647 *Harper's Bazaar.* Ed. Carmel Snow. 86 (2,902) (September 1953).

Written on front cover: "p. 234." Includes O'Connor's "A Late Encounter with the Enemy," pp. 234, 247, 249, 252; biographical note, p. 96.

Letters, pp. 43, 44, 48, 65, 66.

648 ———. 91 (2,960) (July 1958).

Signed on front cover. Includes O'Connor's "The Enduring Chill," pp. 44–45, 95, 96, 100–102, 108; biographical note, p. 31.

Letters, pp. 264, 271, 273, 293, 575.

649 *Holiday.* Ed. Ted Patrick. 30 (3) (September 1961).

Includes O'Connor's "Living with a Peacock," pp. 52–53, 110–12, 114.

Letters, pp. 405, 408, 411, 433, 447.

650 ———. Copy 2

651 ———. Copy 3.

652 *Integrity.* Ed. Edward Willock and Carol Johnson. 4 (3) (December 1949).

Signed "Ethel [Daniell]" on cover. "Detachment" written on front cover.

For Elizabeth Williams, "Detachment": marginal linings, pp. 37, 39, 44; underlinings, pp. 37, 44.

653 ———. 8 (3) (December 1953).

For "Mrs. Candle," "He Married an Angel": marginal linings, pp. 7, 8, 11; marginalia: "priceless!" p. 7.

654 *Jubilee*. Ed. Edward Rice. 9 (1) (May 1961).

On front cover: "p–28." Includes O'Connor's "Mary Jane," pp. 28–35; biographical note, p. 1.

Letters, pp. 423, 429, 441.

655 ———. Copy 2.

656 *The Kenyon Review*. Ed. John Crowe Ransom. 15 (1) (Winter 1953).

657 ———. 15 (2) (Spring 1953).

Signed on front cover. Includes O'Connor's "The Life You Save May Be Your Own," pp. [195]–207. Marginal linings and question marks next to the following passages: p. 200, lines 11–12; p. 205, lines 14–15; p. 207, lines 16–17, 31–32. Also includes review of *Wise Blood* by Joe Lee Davis, pp. 320–22.

Letters, pp. 48–49, 50, 66, 148.

658 ———. 15 (3) (Summer 1953).

659 ———. 15 (4) (Autumn 1953).

Review of Russell Kirk, *The Conservative Mind: From Burke to Santayana* (see entry 251), pp. [648]–54.

660 ———. 16 (1) (Winter 1954).

661 ———. 16 (2) (Spring 1954).

Written on front cover: "p. 169." Includes O'Connor's "A Circle in the Fire," pp. 169–88. Underlining, p. 185, line 16; check marks, p. 185, lines 22, 24, 27; corrections: "fall" changed to "wall," p. 170, line 12; "muttered" changed to "suggested," p. 178, line 30; "some" checked, last word on p. 173.

Letters, p. 70.

662 ———. 17 (2) (Spring 1955).

Includes O'Connor's "The Artificial Nigger," pp. 169–92. Corrections: "N" for "negro," p. 179, line 31; "but" changed to "and," p. 181, line 23; "roms" changed to "rows," p. 182, line 10.

663 ———. Copy 2.

664 ———. Copy 3.

665 ———. 17 (4) (Autumn 1955).

Reviews of Vivas, *Creation and Discovery: Essays in Criticism and Aesthetics* (see entry 288), pp. [633]–39; of Welty, *The Bride of the Innisfallen and Other Stories* (see entry 611), pp. 661–64; of O'Connor, *A Good Man Is Hard to Find*, pp. 664–70.

666 ———. 18 (3) (Summer 1956).

Signed on front cover; "p. 384" on front cover. Includes O'Connor's "Greenleaf," pp. 384–410.

Letters, pp. 146, 148–49, 181, 192, 575.

667 ———. Copy 2.

668 ———. 19 (4) (Autumn 1957).

669 ———. Ed. Robie Macauley. 21 (3) (Summer 1959).

Review of Lowell, *Life Studies* (see entry 358), pp. 482–88.

670 ———. 21 (4) (Autumn 1959).

Letters, p. 356.

671 ———. 22 (4) (Autumn 1960).

Includes O'Connor's "The Comforts of Home," pp. 523–46.

Letters, pp. 371, 375, 416, 575.

672 ———. Copy 2.

673 *The Month.* N.S. 10 (5) (November 1953).

Written on front cover: "p 284."

For W. Peters, "The Concern of Graham Greene": underlining, p. 284.

674 *Northwest Review.* Ed. Edward van Aelstyn. 5 (2) (Spring 1962).

On front cover: "p 89." Letter enclosed reads: "March 7

62 Dear Flannery: I thought you might enjoy 'Graduate Snapshots.' Marion Montgomery." Montgomery's story of that name is on pp. 89–93.

675 *Partisan Review.* Ed. William Phillips and Philip Rahv. 16 (2) (February 1949).

Signed on front cover. Includes O'Connor's "The Heart of the Park," pp. 138–51.

Letters, pp. 4, 5, 6, 17, 21.

676 ———. 23 (4) (Fall 1956).

Catherine Carver is Assistant Editor.

Letters, p. 80.

677 ———. 24 (1) (Winter 1957).

678 ———. 24 (2) (Spring 1957).

679 ———. 24 (3) (Summer 1957).

680 ———. 24 (4) (Fall 1957).

Signed on front cover. "Matthew 7–1" written on cover. Includes O'Connor's "A View from the Woods," pp. [475]–96. Textual correction: "whom" changed to "who," p. 479, line 30.

Letters, pp. 181, 186, 250, 268, 575.

681 *Perspectives USA.* 14 (Winter 1956).

Includes O'Connor's "The Life You Save May Be Your Own," pp. [64]–75.

682 ———. Copy 2. British edition.

683 ———. Copy 3. French edition.

Includes O'Connor's "Sauver Sa Vie," pp. [80]–91.

684 *PMLA (Publications of The Modern Language Association of America).* Ed. George Winchester Stone, Jr. 78 (5) (December 1963).

Written on front cover: "villians and non-villians—Hawthorne pg 551."

685 *Ramparts.* Ed. Edward M. Keating. 1 (5) (March 1963).

Annotations by Janet McKane on table of contents (p. 1): "For Flannery" at top; check marks against two essays on art and next to "A Symposium on Jesuit University Education" with comment "mostly true I think."

For Wallace Fowlie, "Julien Green": marginal linings on pp. 83, 86, 87, 88, 89, 90.

"Since the death of Bernanos, and since the last major novels of Mauriac, Julien Green is the one French novelist today whose books testify to the real presence of God in His apparent absence" (marginal lining, p. 83).

"Wilfred, a young American of twenty-four, living in the South, has a sincere profound faith. He is a Catholic in a Protestant milieu" (part of a marginal lining, p. 88).

686 *Renascence: A Critical Journal of Letters.* 16 (1) (Fall 1963).

For Brainard Cheney, "Caroline Gordon's Ontological Quest": brackets, p. 11; circled words (typographical errors), pp. 4, 5, 7, 11.

687 *St. Jude.* Ed. Rev. Robert J. Leuver, C.M.F. 27 (11) (March 1962).

Written on front cover: "page 7—Memoir of Mary Ann." Includes O'Connor's "A Memoir of Mary Ann," pp. 7–11.

688 ———. Copy 2.

689 *The Sewanee Review.* Ed. J. E. Palmer. 56 (2) (Spring 1948).

Signed "F. O'Connor" on front cover. Includes O'Connor's "The Train," pp. [261]–71.

Letters, p. 4.

690 ———. Ed. Monroe K. Spears. 61 (3) (Summer 1953).

Signed on front cover. Includes O'Connor's "The River," pp. [455]–75.

Letters, pp. 48, 60.

691 ———. 63 (2) (Spring 1955).

Written on front cover: "p. 204."

For J. A. Bryant, Jr., "Shakespeare's Allegory: *The Winter's Tale*": marginal lining, p. 204; marginalia: "how much dogma left operative now?" p. 204.

692 ———. Ed. Andrew Lytle. 70 (3) (Summer 1962).

Includes O'Connor's "The Lame Shall Enter First," called a novella on cover, pp. [337]–79; Robert Fitzgerald, "The Countryside and the True Country," on "The Displaced Person," pp. [380]–94; and John Hawkes, "Flannery O'Connor's Devil," pp. [395]–407. Marginal linings on pp. 396, 397, 398, 399, 400, 402, 403, 406; marginalia: "?" p. 402.

Letters, pp. 453, 455–57, 460, 461, 464, 470–71, 475, 486, 500, 507, 575.

693 ———. Copy 2.

694 ———. 72 (2) (Spring 1964).

Includes O'Connor's "Revelation," pp. [178]–202.

Letters, pp. 560, 563, 569, 574, 575, 578, 590.

695 ———. Copy 2.

696 ———. Copy 3.

697 *Shenandoah.* Ed. T. H. Carter. 4 (1) (Spring 1953).

Includes "A Stroke of Good Fortune," pp. [7]–18, with the following passage crossed out on p. 15:

" 'I just asked you what it was.'

'It was a boil,' Ruby said sullenly. 'A nigger told me what to do and I did it and it went off. I'd do that for whatever I got now only this town is too big; you can't get the things.'

'What things?'

'Just things. What do you think you know? What do you. . . .' "

698 ———. Copy 2.

Ford Madox Ford, "Observations on Technique" checked on front cover; pp. 43–50, including Ford essay, missing.

699 ———. Copy 3.

700 ———. Ed. Marshall W. Fishwick. 13 (1) (Autumn 1961).

701 *The Sign.* Ed. Rev. Ralph Gorman, C.P. 42 (2) (September 1962).

For table of contents: check mark, asterisks, underlining, p. 9.

For Hans Küng, "The Mass of the Future": marginal linings, p. 21; check marks, pp. 20, 21.

For Sr. M. Dominic, R.G.S., "A Friend for Neurotic": marginal lining, p. 57.

702 *Tematy.* 22 (6) (Winter 1963).

Includes O'Connor's "A Circle in the Fire," pp. 87–108, in Polish.

703 *Thought.* Ed. William F. Lynch, S.J. 29 (112) (Spring 1954).

Signed on cover. Review of Crane, *Critics and Criticism: Essays in Method* (see entry 320), pp. 145–52.

For William F. Lynch, "Theology and the Imagination": marginal linings, pp. 63, 64, 65, 68, 82; underlinings, pp. 65, 66, 67, 70, 71, 77, 81, 82; marginalia: "Tillich?" p. 66; "i.e. the classical," p. 66.

"Wherever in the West tragedy had ever come off well, the achievement of it was due to: 1. a doctrine of the profundity of existence and 2. a sense of the failure of human energy to enter into an equation with it. Wherever it has come off badly it is because these terms have been revered: 1. existence is absurd, mean or flat (manichaean); 2. man becomes the romantic hero (the Pelagian), conquering mystically and irrationally by rebellion, resentment or exaltation in pain. We could easily establish this in terms of such people as O'Neill, Anderson, Odets, Paul Green, Williams, Miller, Lawson, Irwin Shaw, Sartre, Malraux and even Eliot" (marginal lining, p. 63).

"Only, we must take a more positive stand toward the elements of total predecision which make each of us the kind of explorer of the world of symbol and being that we are. We must all of us decide that our dogmas are instruments of exploration into the real, and that the latter does not give up its secrets to those who have no instruments. Surely the new image will take on the analogical shape of the old, but that does not allow any man to say in advance what the next piece of history, the next fact, the next image, will be that confronts him, or what the analogical shape or rhythm it will be given" (marginal lining, second sentence underlined, p. 65).

"The matter, therefore, of the fixity of dogma has no relevance whatsoever for the poet; but whether dogma fixes or frees the imagination has every conceivable relevance for him" (marginal underlining, p. 65).

". . . the analogical as that habit of perception which sees that different levels of being are also somehow one and can therefore be *associated in the same image,* in the same and single act of perception. We may lump together under the word 'manichaean' all those habits of perception which instinctively *dissociate*" (underlined, annotated "Tillich?" p. 66).

"Christianity has from the beginning demanded that the search for redemption and the infinite be through the finite, through the limited, through the human" (underlining, p. 71).

"And that is largely because it is not so constructed that the secret of anything is located at any one absolutely single center" (entire passage underlined, p. 77).

"Literally, it is open to narrative. I conceive that this is what is present in Dante, who does not know what the next monster will be nor what the next decision, except in some analogical mode. And since the possibilities are as large as history itself, the historical imagination is infinitely freer than the analytical. For there is always an end to the latter, especially to what we might call the purely psycho-analytic imagination. Does not the good analyst himself lead the patient to confront event?" (marginal lining, and partly underlined, p. 82).

Letters, p. 132.

704 ———. 33 (125) (Summer 1957).

Signed on top of first page (p. 161).

Denis A. Goulet's "Kierkegaard, Aquinas, and Abraham" and Joseph F. Costanzo's "Religious Syncretism in India" checked on cover.

Letters, pp. 241, 273.

705 ———. 33 (28) (Spring 1958).

Review of Vawter, *A Path through Genesis* (see entry 98), pp. 153–54.

For Yves M.-J. Congar, "The Idea of Conversion": marginal lining, p. 13.

"One may say of it [conversion] what Kierkegaard says of faith: 'Belief is not an understanding like another, one more qualification applied to the same individual (we would add: an idea of a new system of ideas); no, risking belief, man himself becomes another' " (marginal lining, p. 13).

706 ———. 36 (141) (Summer 1961).

Review of Teilhard, *The Divine Milieu: An Essay on the Interior Life* (see entry 65), pp. 289–91.

707 ———. 37 (147) (Winter 1962).

Signed on cover. Review of Dillistone, *The Novelist and the Passion Story: A Study of Christ Figures in Faulkner, Mauriac, Melville, and Kazantzakis* (see entry 338), pp. 616–18.

For Christopher F. Mooney, "Blondel and Teilhard de Chardin: An Exchange of Letters": marginal linings, pp. 545, 547, 548, 549; brackets, pp. 544, 549; underlinings, pp. 544, 545, 548; check point, p. 551; marginalia: question mark, p. 545; "1919," p. 550.

"Thus in spite of our attachment to things we shall become detached. In fact it is our very attachment which will detach us, because in the sphere of nature itself there is a power of renunciation, a 'creative' death, which is really the beginning of that renunciation imposed by Christ on every member of His Body" (marginal lining, p. 549).

". . . the natural order is characterized by a radical instability; the whole is tending nevertheless toward Christ who is even now Center of His Plenitude. The new cosmos is not to be created beside the old but is to proceed from its transformation" (marginal lining and brackets, p. 549).

708 *Tomorrow.* Ed. Eileen J. Garrett. 8 (12) (August 1949).

Signed "O'Connor" on cover. Includes O'Connor's "Woman on the Stairs" (revised, "A Stroke of Good Fortune"), pp. 40–44.

709 *U.S. Catholic.* Ed. Rev. Robert J. Leuver, C.M.P. 19 (9) (January 1964).

Includes O'Connor's "Everything That Rises Must Converge," pp. 12–18.

710 ———. Copy 2.

711 ———. Copy 3.

712 ———. Copy 4.

Annotation by Janet McKane on cover: "pg–12 'Everything That Rises Must Converge.' "

Index

Listed below are the authors, editors, translators, and illustrators of materials in Flannery O'Connor's personal library. The numbers following the names refer to entry numbers. An asterisk (*) denotes direct quotation. Significant annotations are also included.